CHURCHILL

THE LIFE TRIUMPHANT

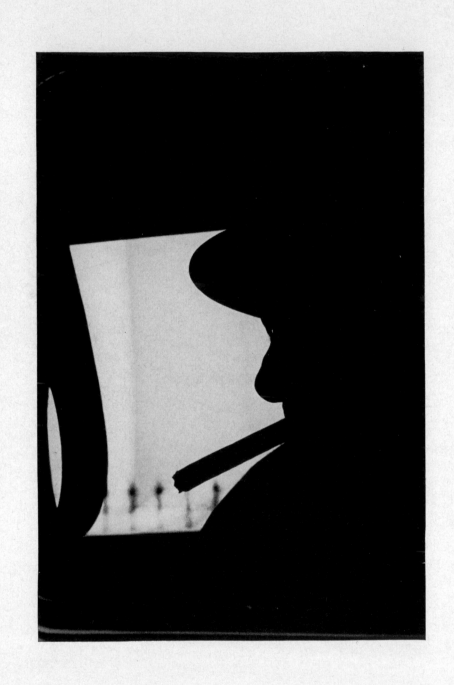

CHURCHILL

THE LIFE TRIUMPHANT

THE HISTORICAL RECORD OF NINETY YEARS

compiled by

AMERICAN HERITAGE MAGAZINE

and

UNITED PRESS INTERNATIONAL

with a biographical essay by

HENRY ANATOLE GRUNWALD

and

an introduction by

DWIGHT D. EISENHOWER

Published by AMERICAN HERITAGE PUBLISHING CO., INC.

SIR WINSTON CHURCHILL
A PERSONAL VIEW

By DWIGHT D. EISENHOWER

On the eve of the Nazi invasion of Poland in September, 1939, Winston Churchill —his sixty-fifth birthday a little more than three months off—could look back on a long lifetime distinguished by more success in more careers than could most men of his age.

He had been a combat soldier on the Empire's far frontiers; a political leader not bound to partisan machines, for he had changed party affiliations when conviction so dictated; a principal architect of Britain's naval greatness in World War I; a strategist of that war whose daring plan, if it had been daringly executed, might have saved many millions of lives; a newspaper correspondent and author whose works in history and in biography had won him enduring fame.

In that season of 1939, his present was controversial and his future obscure: he was the prophet unheeded. Through the years, sometimes almost alone, his voice had been raised in warnings against Nazi aggression, in pleas that Britain prepare for war total beyond human experience. His warnings were soon fully to be realized, although his pleas had been inadequately answered.

Within a few weeks, however, he would return to the Admiralty and the office he had first assumed almost thirty years before. Nine months later, as Britain faced up to the darkest hours in its history, he became war leader of a beleaguered kingdom and its dominions beyond the sea.

Through three years of war, we were in constant association. So long as my headquarters were in England, preparing for the invasion of North Africa and, later, the liberation of the European continent, we met formally twice each week: for Tuesday lunch at 10 Downing Street; and for Friday evening discussions that often continued into the morning, either there or at Chequers, the Prime Minister's country place. On occasion we went together on extensive inspection tours among Allied troops.

But the man, at once so restlessly impatient at getting things done personally and so eager for information at first-hand, could not abide by any fixed schedule. Often, unheralded, he descended on me to present a new idea, to argue once again a rejected proposal, to get the latest word on battle—or just to chat.

Through my wartime association with him, the whole globe seemed to be an exercise ground for a mind that could, almost in the same instant, wrestle with an immediate problem in the deployment of air and land and sea forces and probe into the far-off future, examining the coming peacetime role of the embattled nations, shaping for his listener the destiny of the world.

Forever conscious of his responsibilities on the world scene and of his place in world history, Winston Churchill was, nevertheless, devoid of pompous stuffiness or of indifference to those about him. When Nazi planes swept up the Thames estuary on a raid over London, his habit was, when duty permitted, to search out his daughter Mary, a sergeant in an antiaircraft battery, and assure himself of her safety. At other times, he would visit the burning districts, heartening and encouraging the homeless survivors of the raid. His siren suit on those occasions, that might well have made any other man a ridiculous figure, became a symbol of Londoners' ability to withstand the terror of fire bomb and blockbuster.

The immensity of his energy, of his devotion to a cause, of his scorn for those who despaired, and of his faith in Britain were daily manifest throughout the war. At all times he seemed to be Britain itself; by those around him and even by his deadliest enemies in the Axis camp he was so recognized. Seldom in history has one man so greatly symbolized a race of men and women, their strengths and their loyalties. But the stature of his leadership was not solely a creation of war.

When he had passed the biblical three score years and ten, rejected in his political leadership by the people he had led to victory, he moved against a new challenge. His party crushed, the aging Churchill took on the heavy task of rebuilding its ranks and restoring it to national power. The political saga of those years, quieter in tone and less dramatic in its movements and maneuvers, was as Churchillian in its tale of ultimate triumph as the saga of war. He became in 1951, once again, Britain's Prime Minister.

After I had been elected President, I was privileged to be associated with him in problems of world-wide scope, both of us still working in support of freedom and in opposition to all forms of tyranny. In personal conversation face to face and in many trans-Atlantic phone calls, I found him, despite the weight of years, still a source of inspiration, of wisdom, above all of faith that right and justice firmly maintained will ever triumph.

Half American by ancestry and citizen of all the free world by the leadership he gave it, Winston Churchill was the authentic Englishman all his days.

Neither England nor the world shall soon look upon his like again.

Dwight Eisenhower

MAN OF THE CENTURY

By HENRY ANATOLE GRUNWALD

"It is fun to be in the same decade with you," Franklin Roosevelt wrote to a great friend in the early 1940's, thereby committing a magnificent understatement. For it was, more accurately, an inspiration and an adventure to be in the same century with Winston Churchill.

No other career dominates that century as does his. And yet—it may be a lesson in irony, in patience, or in fate—the century was nearly half gone before Churchill truly came into his own. Sir Harold Nicolson recalls meeting him at a country house in 1908. Though he was only thirty-four and already a Cabinet minister, Churchill was showing some petulance about the delays he encountered in office. "But surely," someone said, "You have no need to be in such a hurry. . . . You have years before you." "Oh, but I do need to hurry," answered the young minister, "you see, all we Churchills damp off after the age of forty."

Winston Churchill had been a public figure in England since the age of twenty-five, but his early life was shadowed by the memory of his father, Lord Randolph Churchill, the political prodigy who before he reached forty found his bright career in sudden and total eclipse. The son's deep sense of historic parallel in this case played him false—but it may have forewarned him against the political perils ahead.

When Winston Churchill himself was forty he was brilliantly successful as First Lord of the Admiralty, the minister responsible for bringing the British Fleet to readiness for World War I. But six months later he was driven from office, saddled with blame for the failure of the Gallipoli campaign. More than twenty-five years elapsed before he reached such a peak again, and for the last ten of those years he was a voice unheeded—a voice which became the greatest in the free world, warning against the rise of Nazi Germany. He was sixty-five when he was called at last to lead the nation, but the crisis made him "feel twenty years younger," and he could say with utter confidence: "I thought I knew a good deal about it all, and I was sure I should not fail." On the eve of another struggle for survival, two centuries earlier, the elder William Pitt, Earl of Chatham, had merely been more candid: "I know that I can save this country and that no one else can."

Winston Churchill was perhaps the last great man of the West—the West as we have known it. He was not destined to guide or witness great beginnings. In his versatile genius he was the most Elizabethan of modern statesmen, and like Drake, the model Elizabethan, he preserved Britain in a moment of supreme peril. But he could not, like Drake, sail toward new horizons. Like Chatham, who led England in the Seven Years' War, he was a martial minister, commanding his commanders and rallying his nation. But he could not, like Chatham, win a new empire. Like the younger Pitt, who doggedly fought Napoleon, he tirelessly warred on his continental enemy; and he lived to see the enemy defeated, which was not granted Bonaparte's antagonist. But he could not, like Pitt, expect his country to move into another century of expanding wealth and power.

A matchless leader who might have built and administered

new worlds, Churchill could only rescue the old. The glimpse we have of him as a young lieutenant of the 4th Queen's Own Hussars, stationed in India and reading Gibbon in the afternoon sun, remains one of the most significant vignettes from this rich and varied life. For the British Empire had entered upon its own Decline and Fall. Although Churchill had the gifts of a successful conqueror and the impulses of a generous one, history allowed him to be only a conqueror on the defensive.

But in that role he won a victory more famous than any that can be claimed by the great warrior-statesmen from Alexander to his own ancestor, John Churchill. And of that famous victory, no one can justly ask, like the child in Southey's poem, "But what good came of it at last?"

To a new generation, the good that came of Nazi Germany's defeat is perhaps no longer immediately and passionately clear. In a world which is already partially governed by men who were only children when Winston Churchill was the leader of Britain, the danger of those days has already begun to recede into the remoteness of textbooks. Yet the overwhelmingly simple facts remain: Nazi Germany was a ghastly cancer that had to be killed if the West, indeed the world, were not to be devoured; and Winston Churchill more than any other man killed Nazi Germany. What if he had failed? The imagination is hard-pressed to supply the picture. But surely the difference would have gone far beyond the customary consequences of victory or defeat in the customary rivalries among nations. Surely the difference would have been more on the order of what happened when Athens fell to Sparta, or what would have happened had Europe fallen to the Turks: a major break in the West's long and troubled story.

With his keen, not to say theatrical, grasp of history, Churchill understood the significance of his long career and its extraordinary climax better than anyone. He first served the Crown under Queen Victoria and still did under Queen Elizabeth II. He linked the age of cavalry to the age of rockets, the era of *laissez faire* to the era of the welfare state. Through half a century of public life, he failed in politics as often as he succeeded, he rebelled more often than he obeyed, he was vilified more often than he was cheered. He was perhaps never entirely trusted—except in that final extremity when Britain unquestioningly turned to him and placed herself wholly in his hands.

Churchill's most important service to his nation, and to the free world, was inspirational. Throughout World War II, he spoke for Britain in a way in which no statesman had ever expressed the courage of a people. In this age of the ghost writer, we sometimes tend to think of oratory as a mere ornament of policy, perhaps a slightly vulgar ornament. It is necessary to have sat in a dim room listening to that incomparable voice, at moments when a Nazi victory seemed entirely possible, to understand that Churchill's speeches were not ornamental but, literally, an essential contribution to the war. Nothing else and no one else could so surely buoy up flagging hopes or restore confidence—in Britain and in oneself. As the Swedish Academy put it when he won the Nobel Prize for Literature in 1953, he had "mobilized" the language.

Churchill did not necessarily require the themes of war and glory to bring out his best. He could be cogent, sarcastic, and moving on the gold standard, free trade, Liberalism versus Toryism, or Toryism versus Socialism. But while in peacetime he sometimes sounded a little too Jovian for comfort, he was a perfect spokesman in time of war. As long as the English language endures, his best speeches will endure. For those who heard them, or even heard of them, it still takes only a few cues to start them ringing through the memory: "We shall fight on the beaches, we shall fight on the landing grounds"; "Never in the field of human conflict was so much owed by so many to so few"; "This bloodthirsty guttersnipe"; "What kind of people do they think we are?"; "Some chicken! Some neck!"; "Give us the tools, and we will finish the job"; "Good night then: sleep to gather strength for the morning. For the morning will come"; "This was their finest hour"; and above all, "I have nothing to offer but blood, toil, tears, and sweat." Pedants have pointed out that Livy, Cicero, and Garibaldi, among others, used similar phrases. Which does not change the fact that, as the distinguished British historian A. L. Rowse writes, "Even now . . . with the dust lying upon so much ardor along the dreary way, one can hardly see for tears in transcribing those words that bring back that glorious, unforgettable summer, the long hot days full of catastrophe and suspense, the country's sudden and complete uncovering, the mortal danger we stood in."

It was not only the words that made Churchill the great charismatic leader of World War II; it was the whole sum and style of his life.

Although in some quarters he was considered an anachronism, it was suddenly right to have him on hand to embody so much of Britain's history. The mere outline of his military service reads like a roll call of the past: he had served, apart from the 4th Hussars, in the 31st Punjabs, the 21st Lancers, the South African Light Horse, the Oxfordshire Yeomanry, the 2nd Grenadier Guards, the 6th Royal Scots Fusiliers, and the Oxfordshire Artillery. His record in government was even longer and more varied, and even his failures only served to recall his extraordinary quality of never giving up, of always bouncing back. That special Churchillian mixture of rebelliousness and conservatism, of impertinence and reverence, of changeability and endurance, of gusto for life and contempt for death—all this rose behind his words. When he pledged to fight to the end, there was no question but that he meant it literally, that he fully believed what he later expressed in a magnificent line: "This was a time when it was equally good to live or die."

Throughout the blitz he seemed constantly to be appearing among the ruins, his squat, stooped, but defiant figure striding through the wreckage, cheering the people and being cheered by them. On one such occasion in a particularly poor and hard-hit part of London, Churchill later recalled, he was surrounded by a crowd "manifesting every sign of lively affection, wanting to touch and stroke my clothes. One would have thought I had brought them some fine substantial benefit which would improve their lot in life. I was completely undermined and wept. [General Sir Hastings] Ismay, who was with me, records that he heard an old woman say, 'You see, he really cares. He's crying.'" Churchill never feared to display emotion in public—a quality in which the old aristocrat showed himself, if not un-British, certainly un-middle-class.

He had genius as a leader, statesman, orator, and writer, but one of his greatest talents was being a man—a man both legendary and loved, admirable and amusing, larger than life and closer to earth than most great figures. One cannot consider his achievement in war without first considering his achievement in merely being himself.

The main theme of his character was self-confidence—and, mingled with it, a quality of boyishness. It showed itself in a childhood moment when, while being caned by an older pupil, he managed to say: "I shall be a greater man than you." And it showed itself just as surely as it did during World War II, in his calm, even happy, assumption of total responsibility amid disaster.

The world cherished not only the hero, but the irrepressible *enfant terrible,* the side of him which H. G. Wells described as the "knee-worthy little boy." Seldom has a public person been held at once in so much awe and so much affection, or evoked such fond proprietary chuckles along with blood-stirring thrills of pride. It was part of this double appeal that he could tell his generals how to win battles and also snarl at his throat specialist, "I entirely disagree with your diagnosis"; that he could petulantly say about his farm, "I'm going to make it pay, whatever it costs," and could superbly tell the Germans in the early part of the war, "We shall defend our island, whatever the cost may be."

He set the pattern at the very start by being born in Blenheim Palace—prematurely, while his mother was visiting the ancestral home. At school he was a poor pupil, yet he displayed a spirit both mischievous and indomitable. It has become part of the Churchill legend that a Latin teacher once tried to enlighten him about the vocative case by explaining that *mensa* meant " 'O table' . . . you would use it in speaking to a table"; Winston remarked innocently, "But I never do." When, on another occasion, the headmaster informed him that " I have grave reason to be displeased with you," he replied, "And I, sir, have grave reason to be displeased with you." In the opinion of some Old Harrovians, the most courageous thing young Churchill did was to show his nurse lovingly all around the school when she came to visit, braving the jeers of the junior Spartans who were his classmates.

As he failed Latin and kept repeating the same form with its emphasis on "teaching the stupidest boys the most disregarded thing—namely to write mere English," he developed the style that in later years became so masterly and unmistakable. Even his schoolboy writings were impressive, whether he was attacking conditions in the school gym or composing an epic about a flu epidemic on the Continent:

> *And now Europe groans aloud*
> *And 'neath the heavy thunder-cloud*
> *Hushed is both song and dance;*
> *The germs of illness wend their way*
> *To westward each succeeding day*
> *And enter merry France.*

Even in this context, Churchill never overlooked history or the special destiny of England:

> *In Calais port the illness stays,*
> *As did the French in former days,*
> *To threaten Freedom's isle;*
> *But now no Nelson could o'erthrow*
> *This cruel, unconquerable foe,*
> *Nor, save us from its guile.*

The childish pomposity is amusing, but it is also a little more than that. The mature Churchill often sounded pompous, too. His speeches rang with archaic locutions, with verbal pomp and emotional circumstance that no other speaker could have carried off. But they sounded right coming from Churchill, because they were not borrowed; they were part of the man and his genius.

For all his grandiloquence, he retained his impishness, a quality that was to make him, as one biographer said, the "Peter Pan of politics." Once when he was late for a public dinner and found the doors locked, Churchill climbed in through the pantry window to deliver his speech. Even as Prime Minister, when reprimanded by an adviser for doing something rash, he could still say in his small-boy manner: "Please don't scold me, it was such fun." Not that it was ever easy to scold him; as one of his critics remarked, trying to rebuke Winston Churchill was like trying to rebuke a brass band.

In some respects he seemed to change so little between youth and manhood that, in the 1940's, an elderly member of the Carlton Club was heard to mutter as the familiar figure passed: "Isn't that young Churchill? I haven't seen him since the Boer War." Early in his career Churchill rushed to several wars in his dual capacity as subaltern and war correspondent. He was free with his advice to commanders in the field, and he infuriated them, along with practically everyone else, by his cheerful arrogance. When the Boers took him prisoner, he managed to escape, and five months later preceded the British forces into Johannesburg on a bicycle. While they were hunting him, the Boer authorities posted a reward of twenty-five pounds sterling for his capture and circulated a description that said in part: "Walks with a forward stoop, pale appearance, red-brownish hair, small and hardly noticeable mustache, talks through his nose, and cannot pronounce the letter 'S' properly." Much later when, as Colonial Secretary, he carried on negotiations with Southern Ireland, the Irish leader Michael Collins complained that the British had put a price on his head. "At any rate it was a good price—five thousand pounds," said Churchill. "Look at me—twenty-five pounds dead or alive. How would you like that?"

He was dashing to a degree that, in a lesser man, would have verged on caricature. Before he resigned his commission to devote himself full time to writing and politics, he rejoined his regiment in India, mostly to play in a crucial polo tournament against the 4th Dragoon Guards. Although he had a dislocated shoulder at the time, he led his side to victory. Even after he left the army, Churchill retained a passion for military matters—and when there were none at hand, he easily turned civilian matters into military ones. As Home Secretary he took part personally in the famous "Siege of Sidney Street," when some burglars suspected of being anarchists barricaded themselves in a building in the East End of London and troops were called out to dislodge them. Wearing top hat and fur-lined coat, Churchill oversaw operations. As a contemporary journalist described it: "Peeping round corners he exposed himself with the Scots Guard to the random fire of the besieged burglars, or consulted with his 'staff' in tones of utmost gravity. . . . He agreed that it might be an excellent thing to have in reserve a couple of field guns from the Royal Horse Artillery depot at St. John's Wood, and that a party of Royal Engineers from Chatham might be useful if mining operations had to be undertaken against the citadel." With the same insistence that he must always be on the scene, he proposed to observe the Normandy invasion from a British warship off the coast, overruled General Eisenhower's objection, and gave up only when the King himself intervened. He was fearless, and he had so many narrow escapes that he came to believe that he was "watched over," held in reserve by fate for some special mission.

He had inexhaustible energy, but he also knew how to conserve his resources through never neglecting his comfort. Even during World War I, he had a tin bathtub at the front—scalloped, someone observed, like the shell of Venus —and in Prohibition days his contract for an American lecture tour required a bottle of champagne before each appearance. In World War II, Churchill would stay in bed half the morning, dictating from amid the pillows those memoranda and telegrams on which the fate of the war—and perhaps of the world—so often depended. He would nap in the afternoon and then, restored, work most of the night, forcing his weary staff to keep pace. His official country residence, Chequers, had its own antiaircraft artillery, which Churchill referred to as "my flak." He sometimes called the crew into the house to watch movies, and the British writer Eric Ambler, who served in the crew, recalls Churchill rehearsing one of his speeches while at the same time delightedly watching his screen favorite, Deanna Durbin. He lived well and was served well, and considered both facts entirely natural; once, arriving at the house of a friend on the French Riviera, he exclaimed in wonderment that he had just done the most extraordinary thing: "I came here all the way from London without a servant." He was never reticent about discussing his pleasures. Recalling a certain important experiment he conducted during his soldiering days, he wrote: "By the end of these five days I had completely overcome my repugnance to the taste of whisky. Nor was this a momentary acquirement. On the contrary the ground I gained in those days I have firmly entrenched, and held throughout my whole life."

His inner sense of dignity was so secure that he never required its outer affirmation—hence the eccentric headgear and costumes, which on almost anyone else would have seemed ludicrous. At one shoot arranged by the Duke of

Westminster, Churchill appeared in a hat of his own design—sickly green, with a pork-pie crown and a kind of upturned flap brim. He could look majestic in the robes of a Knight of the Garter or woolly and bearlike in a "siren suit." On a wartime mission to Washington, whose purpose seemed somewhat uncertain, one of Britain's leading soldiers described Churchill sitting in the airplane "dressed in his zip suit and zip shoes with a black Homburg hat on the side of his head and a small gold-topped malacca cane in his hand. Suddenly, almost like Pooh Bear, he started humming, 'We're here because we're here—We're here because we're here.'"

The story goes that at the White House, Roosevelt came to his room and found him stark naked, only to be waved in with the assurance: "The Prime Minister of Great Britain has nothing to hide from the President of the United States." Churchill later denied this, noting that he never received the President without at least a bath towel around his middle. Totally unself-conscious about his appearance, he would wade happily in mud or water as he pursued his hobbies of laying bricks and building goldfish ponds on his estate at Chartwell. An English poet recalls Churchill arriving at the homemade swimming pool one afternoon wearing a Roman toga and a sombrero, which he took off and hung on a bush. He flung himself into the water, rather frightening the poet's young daughter, who was in the pool at the time, and executed "a series of perfectly inexplicable front and back somersaults. Then he got out, took up his toga, and disappeared toward the house."

He was well aware that he had the aspect of a scowling cherub, for when a lady informed Churchill that her baby looked like him, he remarked, "Madam, all babies look like me." David Lloyd George recalled that when Churchill's daughter Diana was born, he proudly proclaimed her "the prettiest child ever seen." "Like her mother, I suppose?" asked Lloyd George. "Not at all," replied Winston, "she is the very image of me." While his massive self-assurance extended to his appearance, it was most formidable in matters of intellect and judgment. It could never be shaken by setbacks, and he had very little reticence about showing it. In Churchill's days as a young politician, the editor of the *Morning Post* allowed him to look over a report of one of his speeches before it went to press, and was startled by what seemed like sudden modesty when Churchill struck out the word "Cheers" at the end of the quotation. But he merely substituted, "Loud and prolonged applause."

As he grew older, he could be brusque, bitter, and downright rude. His invective often had Commons in an uproar.

Attacking the Socialist Prime Minister Ramsay MacDonald for being a political weakling, Churchill recalled that as a child he had been taken to the circus and had wanted most to see the freak known as the Boneless Wonder. "My parents judged that that spectacle would be too revolting and demoralising for my youthful eyes, and I have waited fifty years to see the Boneless Wonder sitting on the Treasury Bench." Gandhi he described as "a seditious Middle Temple lawyer now posing as a fakir." He would interrupt Commons debates with coughs, snarls, stage whispers, and all kinds of distracting gestures. Once an opponent was so irritated by this that he paused in mid-speech to say, "I see my right honourable friend shaking his head. I wish to remind him that I am only expressing my own opinion." "And I wish to remind the speaker," Churchill replied, "that I am only shaking my own head."

Despite his polemics, he was not a hater. Too much of an Olympian to like backslapping conviviality, he nevertheless exuded an air of growling camaraderie that enfolded friends and enemies. His barbs, in their way as classic as his speeches, always had wit and sometimes warmth. Once George Bernard Shaw, an admirer, sent Churchill a pair of tickets to the opening of one of his plays with the note: "Come to my play and bring a friend, if you have a friend." Churchill replied: "I'm busy for the opening, but I'll come to the second night, if there is a second night." Early in his military career, when his face was still decorated in a way dear to many British officers, he sat at dinner next to an outspoken lady who declared: "Young man, I care for neither your mustache nor your political opinions." "Madam," Churchill replied, "you are as unlikely to come into contact with the one as with the other."

He was never idle. The years out of office were the years when he wrote his great historical works, including the brilliant account of the Second World War, the *History of the English-Speaking Peoples,* and the life of the Duke of Marlborough. He was a moralizing historian, who loved to point to the wicked being punished—no one else in the twentieth century could so naturally and convincingly use the word "wicked"—and the just being rewarded. He was also an intensely personal historian. His family feelings about the Duke were so strong that he long refused to undertake the contemplated biography because he feared that he might have to present his great but opportunistic ancestor as something of a scoundrel; he began work only when he found that a famous letter showing Marlborough in a particularly bad light was, in fact, a forgery, and thereafter proceeded not only to rehabilitate but to glorify him.

His dearest and most healing form of relaxation was painting, which he started one summer when he picked up a child's set of water colors. He was addicted to the fiercest, boldest strokes and to the brightest colors. "I rejoice with the brilliant ones," he said, "and am genuinely sorry for the poor browns." Sir John Rothenstein, director of the Tate Gallery, recalled that the amateur painter—who he thought had considerable talent—once told him: "If it weren't for painting, I couldn't live; I couldn't bear the strain of things."

Such moments of pessimism were rare and, particularly in the war, never public. He knew the buoyant influence he had on the British people, so much so that once when he left his residence without his customary cigar, he sent an aide back to get it, explaining, "They expect to see it." Years later when he was honored on his eightieth birthday, Churchill remarked: "I have never accepted what many people have kindly said, namely, that I inspired the nation. Their will was resolute and remorseless and, as it proved, unconquerable. It fell to me to express it, and if I found the right words, you must remember that I always earned my living by my pen and by my tongue. It was the nation and the race dwelling round the globe that had the lion's heart. I had the luck to be called upon to give the roar."

He gave much more than the roar. His leadership of the West in World War II really began in World War I, for the two conflicts are inseparably linked. It was World War I which, in fact, brought the nineteenth century to a close and which marked the beginning of Britain's decline as a world power. Toward the end of that spacious and peaceful century after the defeat of Napoleon, Britain had rested on her laurels; and despite the Victorian era's smug belief in progress, the country had not kept pace with the Industrial Revolution as it rushed onward in Germany and in the United States. When World War I came, thanks to the outrageous *hubris* of the major powers, Britain had to beat back the German challenge for supremacy, but in the end could do it only with American aid. These were the new facts of life, the shape of the new century, but it was not easy to see it at the time. By no means infallible as a prophet, Churchill said as late as 1908 that he foresaw no German menace. But he did predict as well that "the wars of peoples will be more terrible than those of kings."

When he was called to the Admiralty in 1911, he did his brilliant best to prepare the British Navy for war. It had been run along such old-fashioned and personal lines that, during a certain international incident, no one could find the war plan covering the situation: the First Sea Lord, out of town, was believed to be carrying it in his pocket. Major reforms had already been started, but it was Churchill—reorganizing the Admiralty structure, pressing for new ships, and, inci-

dentally, cruising about everywhere in his yacht *Enchantress* —who really gave Britain a modern navy. In all this, he relied heavily on his First Sea Lord, the celebrated and crusty Admiral Lord Fisher. Almost as a side line, on his own responsibility, he also sponsored a series of experiments to develop the tank, although this weapon seemed hardly part of a naval arsenal, and he organized a fleet air arm which gave the navy no fewer than fifty planes at the outbreak of the war. Lord Kitchener, not one of Churchill's admirers, was to say later: "There is one thing at any rate they cannot take from you: the Fleet was ready."

As always, Churchill was hankering for military glory, and as always, he acted on impulse. With the Germans advancing rapidly through Belgium, Churchill personally rushed to the front to try to save Antwerp. He threw marines and auxiliary naval troops into the fray, handling them, in the words of one observer, "as though he were Napoleon and they the Old Guard." He even seriously and rather grandiosely suggested that he resign from the Admiralty and be given a military command in the field. Antwerp fell, and Churchill later admitted that, had he been ten years older, he might not have taken the risk. Still, he felt at the time that it had been worth a try, and characteristically he could point out that at least he had acted: "There is always a strong case for doing nothing."

This period offers a typical personal glimpse of Churchill. He had made his speaking debut long before on a music hall stage, leading a noisy rally against temperance attempts to ban the sale of alcohol in theatres, and he was a veteran of many an uproarious election campaign, including one during which a pretty suffragette followed him about ringing a huge bell whenever he tried to speak. With such training he was not easily fazed by any oratorical task. He entertained the illusion, for example, that he spoke passable French, and tried it on and off the platform. At one point during the Belgian crisis, arriving to confer with the Belgian Cabinet, he happened to be dressed in the uniform of Trinity House, a sailors' organization of which he had been made an "elder brother." When his appearance caused puzzlement, he blithely attempted to explain: *"Je suis le frère aîné de la Trinité."* The Belgians got the impression that Churchill was announcing his divinity, as Robert Lewis Taylor reports the incident, and thereafter spoke softly in his presence.

His role in World War I was overshadowed by a far more serious failure than Antwerp: Gallipoli. Churchill persuaded the Cabinet that the only way to avoid a long, disastrous war of position in the West—the kind of war he later scathingly described as "good, plain, straightforward frontal attacks by valiant flesh and blood against wire and machine-guns"— was to force the Dardanelles and turn the German flank.

Had the operation succeeded, it would have knocked Turkey and Bulgaria out of the war, probably kept Russia in it (thereby conceivably preventing the Russian Revolution), and greatly shortened the conflict, with the consequent saving of millions of lives. Churchill called the plan "the hope of the world." There is now widespread agreement that the idea was brilliant but was bungled in the execution. The military services were simply not ready for an amphibious operation whose basic concept was probably a quarter of a century ahead of its time. "You will see," he had said, "that in a matter of this kind *someone* has to take the responsibility. I will do so—provided that my decision is the one that rules." But Churchill did not wholly rule the undertaking, and it was a lesson he afterward almost fanatically remembered: never assume full responsibility without full control. In World War II, when there was occasional criticism of his leadership, he told the House of Commons bluntly that they could dismiss him but not curb him.

Churchill was despised for the costly Dardanelles failure; he was sacked and went to fight as an officer in France. It was an exceptionally depressing period in his life, but as usual he could not stay gloomy for long. He was originally promised a brigade, but wound up with only a battalion. As a politician he was greeted with suspicion by the troops, but he endeared himself quickly when, virtually on arrival, he assembled the officers and announced: "War is declared, gentlemen, on the lice." With characteristic attention to detail, he followed through with a thoroughly researched lecture on the history, nature, and potential vulnerability of the louse.

By 1917 Prime Minister David Lloyd George found more important employment for him and brought him back into the government as Minister of Munitions. Just after the Armistice, he served importantly as Secretary of State for War and for Air, but essentially his leadership was over, not to be resumed until the 1930's when another war was hideously sprouting from the very graves of the first.

For a while Churchill was not sure about the rising Fascist dictatorships on the Continent. He admired and praised Mussolini. "If I had been an Italian," he said in 1927, "I am sure that I should have been wholeheartedly with you from start to finish. . . . [Italy] has provided the necessary antidote to the Russian poison." But if once again he was not an infallible prophet, he was by far the best one in the fatuous and self-blinded Western democracies. Out of office, he became, in the middle and late thirties, the lonely Cassandra of the House of Commons, rejected by his own party even more than by the Opposition, as he warned against the onrush of disaster. He became even more unpopular during the abdica-

tion crisis, in which he championed King Edward VIII—who wanted to marry the divorced Mrs. Simpson—against Stanley Baldwin, standing squarely for hearth and home, constitution and propriety. Churchill acted from a typically Churchillian sense of chivalry toward his monarch, but also plainly in hopes of hurting the Prime Minister politically. In this he miscalculated, and Churchill's prestige fell lower than ever. But he kept denouncing the policies of a government which he had said was "decided only to be undecided, resolved to be irresolute, adamant for drift . . . all-powerful to be impotent." He pleaded for rearmament, for air parity with Germany, for the formation of an alliance against Hitler. Despite his fervent anti-Communism, he even advocated accepting Stalin's offer of an anti-Nazi pact with the West. But many ruling Conservatives still hoped that Hitler could be used as an instrument against the Russians (once Churchill may have hoped so, too, but not any more). The scornful rejection of the Moscow offer led directly to Stalin's nonaggression pact with Nazi Germany, and hence toward war.

After the Nazi annexation of Austria, which the Chamberlain government condoned, Churchill looked back on the years since the Allied triumph in World War I and declared: "If we study the history of Rome and Carthage, we can understand what happened and why. [But] historians a thousand years hence will still be baffled by the mystery of our affairs. They will never understand how a victorious nation, with everything in hand, suffered themselves to be cast so low, and to cast away all that they had gained by measureless sacrifice and absolute victory—gone with the wind!" When Neville Chamberlain brought home his Munich agreement, Churchill called it an "unmitigated defeat"—and was nearly shouted down in Parliament. Some attempts have been made to rehabilitate Chamberlain by suggesting that he was merely trying to buy time at Munich. The fact remains that, with his predecessor Stanley Baldwin, he marked an era of suicidal mediocrity in Britain. As Churchill put it, in a devastating reference to Chamberlain's good record as Minister of Health, "He viewed world affairs from the wrong end of the municipal drainpipe." But later, after the man of Munich died in November, 1940, Churchill spoke of him with charity: "It fell to Neville Chamberlain, in one of the supreme crises of the world, to be contradicted by events, to be disappointed in his hopes, and to be deceived and cheated by a wicked man."

With the outbreak of the war, Churchill returned to the Admiralty after nearly a quarter of a century, and the famous signal went out to all British naval vessels: "Winston is back." With the exception of the monarch's, Churchill's was probably the only first name that was instantly recognized throughout the Empire. After several months of "phony war," mounting military disaster finally swept Chamberlain out of office and brought Churchill to 10 Downing Street. Thus his role in World War I could now be seen as a mere rehearsal, his years in the political wilderness as a mere test of will and patience, all part of the task he was to perform, all indispensable to the leadership he was to give.

Churchill faced a crisis that compressed in a few short weeks or months enough disasters to exhaust a whole career. The Low Countries were gone; France was collapsing. In the kind of gesture he alone was capable of, Churchill offered the French joint citizenship with the British, an offer which in the whole French Cabinet only Paul Reynaud supported; the others, all committed to surrender, sneered that they did not wish to become a British dominion. With the British Expeditionary Force that had been fighting alongside the French now trapped by the advancing Germans, Churchill was forced to try to evacuate the troops from the Continent. Never doubting for a moment that Britain and he would fight on even if the army were lost, Churchill inspired and organized the evacuation of Dunkirk. "We must be very careful not to assign to this deliverance the attributes of a victory," he said afterward. But perhaps more than any naval victory, it marked the apotheosis of the British as a seagoing people, an unforgettable action in which fishing boats and small pleasure craft sailed unhesitatingly alongside the warships, in order to fetch home the British soldiers and preserve them for the fight ahead. Nearly a third of the craft were lost, but the bulk of the army—more than 338,000 men—was saved. One can only speculate whether it could have happened under another British Prime Minister; it did happen under Churchill, and it was his words that rumbled with the engines of those ships and beat with the wind in their sails.

He never really believed that the Germans would be able to invade Britain, but he squarely faced the possibility. Promising that "The vast mass of London itself, fought street by street, could easily devour an entire hostile army," he resolved not to leave the capital or the country, even if the government were forced into hiding. After he delivered his famous "We shall fight on the beaches" address, he covered the microphone, muttering: "And we will hit them over the head with beer bottles, which is about all we have got to work with."

The great turning point came in the air, when the R.A.F. beat off the German Luftwaffe. Denied mastery of the skies over Britain, the Germans were forced to give up their invasion plan. Up to this point in the war, Churchill's leadership is virtually beyond criticism. As John Winant, the American ambassador, was to remark: "It would have taken so few mistakes to bring about defeat; the miracle was how few were made." Churchill took a series of momentous steps: the move to concentrate what remained of the British fighter air force in Britain, rather than squander it in a futile attempt to save an already doomed France; his order to the British Navy to knock out the French warships in harbor at Oran after the French refused to turn them over to Britain, thus keeping them from falling into German hands; the grueling decisions on aircraft priorities, whether to concentrate on fighters or bombers, on escort craft for vital shipping or on attack craft; the obstinate determination, with the hope of future offensives in mind, to reinforce and hold Egypt at all costs, though other theatres were clamoring for arms and Britain herself was barely safe from invasion; the skillful pleas for U.S. aid which brought, from a willing Roosevelt, the destroyers-for-bases deal. All this represented command and courage of the highest order, at a time when Britain was fighting all alone. In his eagerness for action, Churchill probably made a mistake when he stuck to the letter of prior commitments and sent troops to Greece in a vain attempt to hold off the Germans there. But even in the darkest moments he was determined not to wage a purely defensive war; when he learned that contingency plans for an evacuation of Egypt had been circulated, he furiously ordered all copies recalled.

He never lost a certain belief in omens, which in a less imposing man might be called superstition. Once, when he walked into a room where his son-in-law Vic Oliver was playing "The Blue Danube" on the piano, he started to waltz; when Oliver switched to the Chopin "Funeral March," Churchill angrily stalked from the room. But his sense of fate rarely interfered with his sense of humor. On another occasion, when Generals Dwight Eisenhower and Mark Clark came to see him, he interrupted a long night of war talk by producing an ancient rifle and giving a hearth-rug exhibition of how drill had been carried out in Queen Victoria's army.

Many of the professionals complained that he was a tireless amateur strategist who interfered with everything. Interfere he certainly did. Churchill never overruled his Chiefs of Staff when they were united against him, but, as Eisenhower noted, he maintained such close contact with all operations that he was virtually a member of the staff himself. He was, in effect, *strategos autokrator,* and he later recalled in what he surely considered a modest statement: "All I wanted was compliance with my wishes after reasonable discussion."

Out of his War Room came an unending flow of "minutes," memoranda, and telegrams, totaling nearly one million words through the war, on every conceivable subject from major strategic notions to the particulars of soldiers' gear, commando tactics, and the design of landing vessels. He was so fascinated by detail that he wanted to see even the loading reports of supply ships leaving England. With or without the help of his scientific adviser, he was always mentally tinkering with new technical developments. From his suggestion stemmed the floating harbors that were to be used during the Normandy invasion; and though he did not invent them, he was instrumental in launching, among other things, "Window," a device to confuse the enemy radar; "Oboe," a radio instrument to guide bombers; "Pluto," a pipeline under the ocean. His minutes always had style, as may be gathered from a one-line blast addressed to a high civil servant: "Pray remember that the British people is no longer able to tolerate such lush disorganization." Delay infuriated him, and "Action this day" was his favorite instruction. As to the quality of his orders and suggestions, General Sir Alan Brooke (later Viscount Alanbrooke), who was Chief of the Imperial General Staff, has observed: "Winston never had the slightest doubt that he had inherited all the military genius of his great ancestor, Marlborough. His military plans and ideas varied from the most brilliant conceptions at the one end to the wildest and most dangerous ideas at the other." On balance, it seems that the brilliant, or at least the sound, conceptions predominated.

His main strategic concern of the war was to strike the "soft underbelly of Europe," by which he meant action in the Balkans before a direct assault across the Channel was attempted. This notion was obviously a reincarnation of the Dardanelles idea. In part it was a purely military notion, for Churchill believed in exploiting advantages won in the Mediterranean theatre, and particularly in Italy, where things were not being pressed hard enough to suit his taste. But in part he was also motivated politically, for in a successful campaign to strike at Germany through the Balkans, the Allied armies could have preceded the Red Army into eastern Europe, and thus could have prevented the Russians from establishing Communist regimes there, or at least would have made the process far more difficult. Moscow, of course, wanted no part of that idea. From the start, Stalin clamored for a second front in western Europe, even at a time when the attempt obviously would have been premature and very possibly doomed to failure. The United States, too, favored launching an invasion of France as early as 1942, but thanks largely to Churchill, who kept warning about "rivers of blood" running in the Channel, the project was postponed and the successful invasion of North Africa was launched instead. American commanders came to see the rightness of this decision, but suspicion lingered throughout the war that Churchill was not really in favor of a cross-Channel operation. In fact, he loyally supported the idea, as can be seen from his correspondence, for example, with Field Marshal Jan Smuts. But Churchill wanted to launch the invasion only when preponderant force was available, and in the meantime he kept urging more vigorous Mediterranean actions. Before the assault on Italy, for instance, he criticized what he took to be a too-cautious plan and urged an assault on Rome itself. Contemplating the Italian boot, he wrote: "Why crawl up the leg like a harvest bug from the ankle upwards? Let us rather strike at the knee!"

Strategy and politics became heavily intertwined, which did not surprise Churchill: he once remarked that they are really the same thing, given a high enough angle of vision. Almost instantly after Hitler's invasion of Russia, Churchill had welcomed the Soviets as allies, and in the early months he had done a lot to make that alliance palatable to the West on the irrefutable wartime theory that anyone who was killing Nazis was welcome. Obviously, it was of immense advantage to have the Russians tying down vast numbers of Germans on the eastern front. Nevertheless, Churchill became increasingly dismayed by Stalin's barely disguised intention of seizing as much of Europe as he could after the war. Plans for this were in progress in Moscow when Russia still seemed on the verge of defeat. Moreover, any suggestion that a second front in the West would have to be delayed until the right moment drew withering recriminations from Stalin. On one occasion, when the Russian leader in effect accused the British of cowardice, Churchill unleashed such a tirade of his own that the translator could not keep up. The Americans, on the other hand, were determined to trust the Russians and were sure that Churchill, the old anti-Communist, was exaggerating the difficulties. Two American policies aggravated the situation. The first was Roosevelt's disastrous insistence on a policy of unconditional surrender, accepted by Churchill with some misgivings. The policy was understandable amid the fierce emotions of the time, but Allied readiness to treat with some non-Nazi regime in Germany might have shortened the war and might have avoided the political vacuum which Communism was able to fill in the East. Next, there was the near-insanity of the Morgenthau plan for turning postwar Germany into an agricultural nation, a concept which actually guided Allied occupation policy for a time. Churchill allowed himself to be pressured into accepting the plan, although at first he had rejected it indignantly, because it meant the Allies would be "chained to a dead German for life."

At the Tehran and Yalta conferences, Churchill found himself increasingly isolated from Roosevelt, who did not want America and Britain to gang up on "Uncle Joe" and instead tried to play the moderator between Churchill and Stalin. Thus began a series of disastrous agreements which, among other things, resulted in the loss of Poland to the Communists and bought Russian participation in the war against Japan—which the American military wanted, though it proved to be unnecessary—by giving the Russians territorial and economic concessions in Asia, concessions which played their part later in China's fall to the Reds. These events, of course, must not be judged entirely by hindsight. The Russians, after all, still had enormous military forces committed along the eastern front. The euphoria of wartime alliance—some of it sincere, some artificially engendered—was still strong. And it would be wrong to represent Churchill as the open-eyed, unduped statesman who was dragged into error by the United States. He was not averse to making deals with the Russians himself. At a meeting with Stalin in Moscow in 1944, he worked out a formula for the postwar division of eastern Europe. Jotted down on paper, and approved with a blue mark by Stalin, it went roughly like this:

Rumania—Russian interest	90 per cent
Bulgaria—Russian interest	75 per cent
Greece—British interest (in accord with U.S.A.)	90 per cent
Yugoslavia and Hungary—Russian interest	50 per cent
Other states—Russian interest	50 per cent

"After this," Churchill reported in *Triumph and Tragedy*, "there was a long silence. The penciled paper lay at the center of the table. At length I said, 'Might it not be thought rather cynical if it seemed we had disposed of these issues, so fateful to millions of people, in such an offhand manner? Let us burn the paper.' 'No, you keep it,' said Stalin."

Indeed, the document is revealing, not for any display of cynicism on Churchill's part, but for precisely the opposite. It was naïve to assume that any such percentage deal would be or indeed could be honored by the Russians; the very nature of Communism did not allow it. But in general Churchill did take a far more realistic attitude toward the Russians than did Franklin Roosevelt; and the postwar world would look vastly different if Churchill's views had prevailed. This is particularly true with regard to the events leading up to Potsdam. Despite Churchill's bitter objections, Truman consented to a massive withdrawal from territory already occupied by Allied forces in order to allow Russians in. As Churchill wrote afterward, ". . . to give up the whole center and heart of Germany—nay, the center and key-stone of Europe—as an isolated act seemed to me to be a grave and improvident decision . . . [If] we should go to Potsdam with nothing to bargain with, [then] all the prospects of the future peace of Europe might well go by default." Churchill felt throughout that, much as he admired the Russians' heroic fight and appreciated the advantage it represented to the Western cause, the West was paying heavily for that advantage. The Russians seemed to have the impression, he wrote later, "that they were conferring a great favor on us by fighting in their own country for their own lives. The more they fought, the heavier our debt became." The American government of the period, on the other hand, was far more suspicious of British than of Russian imperialism. At one time, Roosevelt tried to tell Churchill how base were his suspicions. "Winston," he said, "this is something you just are not able to see, that a country might not want to acquire land somewhere even if they can get it."

On balance, Churchill's wartime leadership inevitably calls forth superlatives, but none can possibly compete with Joseph Addison's hymn to Winston's ancestor, the Duke of Marlborough, which happened to be George Washington's favorite poem:

. . . Methinks I hear the drum's tumultuous sound
The victor's shouts and dying groans confound;
The dreadful burst of cannon rend the skies,
And all the thunder of the battle rise.
'Twas then great Marlborough's mighty soul was proved,
That, in the shock of charging hosts unmoved,
Amidst confusion, horror, and despair,
Examined all the dreadful scenes of war:
In peaceful thought the field of death surveyed,
To fainting squadrons sent the timely aid,
Inspired repulsed battalions to engage,
And taught the doubtful battle where to rage.
So when an angel, by divine command,
With rising tempests shakes a guilty land
(Such as of late o'er pale Britannia passed),
Calm and serene he drives the furious blast;
And, pleased the Almighty's orders to perform,
Rides in the whirlwind and directs the storm.

Not all of Winston's wartime commanders may acknowledge these lines as an accurate description of his performance. But if we strip away the literary excess that makes us smile today, and reserve our views as to divine intervention

CONTINUED ON PAGE 28

The heraldic arms of Sir Winston Churchill, K.G., bear the ancient family motto—adopted by the first Sir Winston after his embitterment in the service of King Charles II: "Faithful but unfortunate."

An Ancestral Grandeur

"He was not only the foremost of English soldiers, but in the first rank among the statesmen of our history." Thus Winston Leonard Spencer Churchill summed up the greatness of John Churchill, the first Duke of Marlborough, his ancestor eight generations removed. Pondering what he called the "various long-descending channels" of heredity that produced the Duke, Churchill might well have been thinking of his own descent from the victor of Blenheim. The first duke had left the Churchills a splendid legacy. A military genius who never lost a battle, a commoner who served five sovereigns, he was reckoned, even in his own lifetime, a hero of exalted rank. Enormously wealthy, and enormously proud, he dreamed of a fitting monument: a dynasty of Churchills, housed in a palace and raised above the first families of Europe. Unfortunately, neither of his two sons lived to succeed him. The dukedom passed to the child of a daughter, the heir of the Spencer family. Duke followed duke, each magnificent in his way but none that English history needed to mention. Then the seventh duke, Winston's grandfather, had a nervously brilliant and promising son. The Churchill dynasty, at last, was close to realizing its founder's highest hopes.

John, the first Duke of Marlborough (left), and Sarah, the first Duchess (top), raised the Churchills to fame and nobility.

THE
CHURCHILL
FAMILY
TREE

John Churchill
d. 1659
m.
Sarah Winston

Sir Winston Churchill
1620(?)–1688
m.
Elizabeth Drake

John Churchill
1st Duke of Marlborough
1650–1722
m.
Sarah Jennings

Charles Spencer
3rd Earl of Sunderland
1674–1722

Anne, 2nd daughter of
1st Duke of Marlborough

Henrietta
Duchess of Marlborough
1681–1733

Ambrose Hall
1774–1827
m.
Clarissa Wilcox

Isaac Jerome
1786–1866
m.
Aurora Murray

6th Duke of Marlborough
1793–1857

5th Duke of Marlborough
1766–1840

4th Duke of Marlborough
1739–1817

3rd Duke of Marlborough
1706–1758

Clara Hall

Leonard Jerome
1817–1891

7th Duke of Marlborough
1822–1883

Lady Frances Vane

Jennie Jerome
1854–1921

Lord Randolph Churchill
1849–1895

8th Duke of Marlborough
1844–1892

9th Duke of Marlborough
1871–1934

10th (and present)
Duke of Marlborough
born 1897

John Churchill
1880–1947

Sir Winston Spencer Churchill, K.G., O.M., C.H., C.LIT., F.R.S.
born 1874
m.
Clementine Hozier
born 1885

A Brilliant Father, a Beautiful Mother

Winston's father, Lord Randolph Churchill, works on a state paper, above, in a portrait by Edward Ward.

Few British politicians ever rose as fast as did Winston's father, Lord Randolph Churchill. None ever fell so swiftly. Champion of the working class and a maverick brand of Conservative politics he called "Tory Democracy," Lord Randolph was a national celebrity before he was thirty-five. At thirty-seven he was Chancellor of the Exchequer. Brilliant, eloquent, and daringly independent, Lord Randolph was, however, dangerously flawed for politics. His health was frail, his nerves brittle. Within four months of taking office, he abruptly resigned, expecting to be called back on his own terms. The outraged Conservatives never called. In one afternoon, Lord Randolph's career was finished.

That afternoon was still thirteen years away when Lord Randolph met, and—on their third evening together—proposed to a darkly handsome American heiress named Jennie Jerome. Jennie was the daughter of Leonard Jerome, a New Yorker who had made several fortunes in America's booming Gilded Age and had spent them all in a blaze of high living. What seemed lacking in Lord Randolph, Jennie had in abundance: immense energy, vivacity, and unshakable poise. It has often been said—though never conclusively established—that she was one-sixteenth Iroquois. Their marriage eight months later seemed, in Edmund Burke's phrase, to "bring in the New World to redress the balance of the Old." Within a year, Winston was born, a scion of the Marlboroughs and, it seemed certain, one thirty-second American Indian.

Winston's mother stands intense and lovely in an early formal portrait.
OVERLEAF: *Blenheim Palace, seat of the dukes of Marlborough, stands amid ancient trees. Churchill's parents were visiting the palace when Winston was born, prematurely, in one of the 187 rooms.*

Unruly Child of the Ruling Class

The impromptu delivery room where Winston was born is kept as it was in 1874.

"He is a most difficult child to manage," Lady Randolph reported to her mother. Her redheaded son, who had upset a ball at Blenheim by rushing into the world two months too soon, possessed one marked trait at an early age: a stubborn refusal to be managed by anyone for any purpose he himself did not approve. "I was what grown-up people, in their offhand way, called 'a troublesome boy,'" Churchill explained a half century later. Yet to young Winston, Lady Randolph was a glamorous and awe-inspiring figure. "My picture of her," he recalled, ". . . is in a riding habit, fitting like a skin . . . . My mother always seemed to me a fairy princess . . . . She shone for me like the Evening Star. I loved her dearly—but at a distance." The enemy was nearer—"a sinister figure described as 'the Governess,'" hired, said Churchill, to drag him into a "dismal bog called 'sums.'" He did not go without a fight. One day a maid came to the tutorial room, thinking the governess had rung. "I rang," said Winston. "Take Miss Hutchinson away; she is very cross." He was not yet seven.

Relics of infancy— Winston's curls (right) shorn off when he was five—are preserved in Blenheim. At far right, in one of his earliest portraits, two-year-old Winston leans uncertainly against his mother.

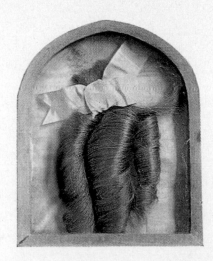

In chubby-faced defiance, at left,
seven-year-old Winston poses in a sailor
suit with practiced aplomb. Above,
Winston at fifteen holds his mother's
arm in a family picture with
his eight-year-old brother, John. Even
at that age, and throughout his quiet
life, John was under the shadow
of Winston's commanding personality.

Reluctant Schoolboy Turned Willing Soldier

Harrow's battered fourth form room, above, held an unhappy and restless Churchill; at right, the out-of-step Harrovian (top) watches from the stairs while schoolmates pose for a group portrait.

Sporting a top hat and cane, fifteen-year-old Churchill, at left, is dressed in the standard Harrow attire. Below, braced in the Spartan uniform of a gentleman-cadet, twenty-year-old Churchill (left) flexes a riding crop alongside two Sandhurst comrades. Soon after, he received his commission and was off to war.

At an age when most schoolboys give up their toy soldiers, young Winston Churchill was still maneuvering his 1,500-man toy army. To adults, it was just one more sign of Winston's backwardness. At school, he was a notable failure. Latin and mathematics—"the subjects," he said, "dearest to the examiners"—he detested, and what he detested he could not learn. At Harrow the son of the former Chancellor of the Exchequer was conspicuous as he marched—in recognition of his academic rank—last in the visitors' day line-up of his form. School days, Churchill later wrote, were "the only barren and unhappy period of my life." His father and his teachers simply thought he was stupid. It was the toy soldiers that changed his life. If nothing else, his father decided, Winston could at least play soldier. At that, it took a desperation course at a "cram" school to squeeze Winston into the famed military college of Sandhurst. Then, suddenly, ten years of failure fell away like a dead husk. Tactics and horsemanship were subjects that made sense to him. His health improved, and his confidence soared. Miscast as a schoolboy, a young man of action emerged from Sandhurst near the top of his class, with little Latin, but with a marvelously keen appetite for adventure.

CONTINUED FROM PAGE 16

in the matter, perhaps we can fairly accept the poem as a summary of Winston Churchill's role in World War II. He did ride the whirlwind; he did direct the storm.

Virtually as soon as the storm abated, in one of the breath-taking reversals of his career, Churchill was dismissed by the electorate. Party rivalry and union demands, long repressed during the years of wartime coalition, now sprouted forth. "The power to shape the future would be denied me," mourned Churchill of his defeat in the 1945 election. One is reminded of Lord Beaverbrook's remark about him on an earlier occasion: "When the government was deprived of his guidance, he could see no hope anywhere." A visitor from the Balkans thought Churchill would be shot; "I have hopes," said Churchill, "that the sentence will be mitigated to a life term at various forms of hard labour." But he was bitter. He declined all honors, including the Garter (which he later accepted, after his retirement). "Why should I accept the Garter from His Majesty," he is said to have remarked, "when his people have just given me the Boot?"

After blood, toil, and tears, Britons understandably enough wanted higher wages, shorter hours, and free eyeglasses. After war, they wanted the welfare state. They were tired of glory and turned away from the figure that symbolized the glory, as well as the suffering, of the past struggle. Above all, there was the old distrust of Churchill, the lingering feeling that his impulsive, ferocious nature made him a great leader for war, but not for peace.

Part of this feeling was due to a certain dazzling inconsistency in Churchill's public positions. He had deserted the Tory party for the Liberals, only to return to the fold later. He had made common cause with Labor, only to attack socialism bitterly. He was a violent foe of Communism, embraced the Communists as allies of war but turned on them again after the war. He had attacked the more benighted imperialists of his youth, and yet remained a die-hard imperialist all his life. "To improve is to change," he said. "To be perfect is to change often." By that standard, he was quite perfect. But frequently his shifts were caused not by changes in his views but by changes in events. He had a sharp instinct for the balance of history, and he sensed more quickly than most when that balance was about to shift. Yet the impression remained that he was inconsistent, and he often seemed out of step with the times, particularly in his attitudes toward three major issues—colonialism, social reform, and Communism.

It is difficult to see how he could have felt very differently about colonialism. He was born a year before Disraeli made

Victoria Empress of India and presented the subcontinent to her, in the words of Winston's father, as "that most truly bright and precious gem in the crown of the Queen." Churchill's first military expedition was under a general incomparably named Sir Bindon Blood, on the North-West Frontier of India, where he combined soldiering and journalism. His romantic nature made him regard the soldiers on the frontier as the "wardens of the marches," and he expressed widespread feeling about the blessings of the white man's burden when he placed some lines by Lord Salisbury on the title page of his early book, *The Story of the Malakand Field Force:* "[Frontier wars] are but the surf that marks the edge and the advance of the wave of civilisation."

Yet Churchill was not blind to the faults and excesses of imperialism. Taking part in the Battle of Omdurman and in the charge against the Dervishes, he was shocked by the desecration of the Mahdi's tomb and by Kitchener's carrying off the prophet's head in a kerosene can. During the Boer War, Churchill was sharply critical of the British command. He warned against underrating the Boers and called for a reorganized force: "There is plenty of work here for a quarter of a million men. Are the gentlemen of England all foxhunting?" After he went into politics and became an Under Secretary of State for the Colonies, he pleaded eloquently for a generous peace with the Boers. After World War I, as full-fledged Colonial Secretary, faced with the vacuum left behind by the crumbled Ottoman Empire, he negotiated a Middle East settlement that, for all its inevitable seeds of future conflict, lasted until World War II. Even Lawrence of Arabia praised Churchill for it. He was active in trying to make Palestine a "national home" for the Jews, but ran into political criticism over his granting an irrigation concession to a Jewish entrepreneur. In Commons, Churchill complained acidly: "It is hard enough in all conscience to make a new Zion, but if, over the portals of the new Jerusalem you are going to inscribe the legend 'no Israelites need apply,' I hope the House will permit me in future to confine my attention exclusively to Irish matters."

He did negotiate the delicate treaty giving independence to Southern Ireland. Yet he was stubborn and misguided about India, whose independence he opposed bitterly to the end. "I have not become the King's First Minister," as he said during the war, "in order to preside over the liquidation of the British Empire."

While his critics realized that this liquidation was inevitable, no matter who presided over it, their views were not always more realistic than his. They held exaggerated and sometimes naïve expectations for the newly freed nations, and in the light of the present, Churchill's own dire predictions of disorder and corruption in India and other freed colonies no longer seem quite as wrong-headed as they did at the time. In general, he seemed less changeable in these matters than in some others. Years ago he said, "We are all Imperialists nowadays. It is not only a political faith, but the prevailing fashion. I am an Imperialist, too—though I do not like the name—and perhaps I shall remain one when it is less fashionable, and from an electioneering point of view less profitable than at present."

Churchill is sometimes accused of having resisted his era's social revolution as much as he resisted the anticolonial revolution. That charge is hardly fair. He started public life in an almost unbelievably different atmosphere from the one in which he ended it. "In those days, English Society still existed in its old form," Churchill himself wrote. "It was a brilliant and powerful body, with standards of conduct and methods of enforcing them now altogether forgotten. In a very large degree every one knew every one else and who they were. The few hundred great families who had governed England for so many generations and had seen her rise to the pinnacle of her glory, were inter-related to an enormous extent by marriage. Everywhere one met friends and kinsfolk. The leading figures of Society were in many cases the leading statesmen in Parliament, and also the leading sportsmen on the Turf. Lord Salisbury was accustomed scrupulously to avoid calling a Cabinet when there was racing at Newmarket, and the House of Commons made a practice of adjourning for the Derby." Churchill did not like all the changes that were taking place, and mourned for some of the great old houses "in whose faded saloons Socialist Governments drearily dispense the public hospitality." But while he essentially remained a nineteenth-century figure, he kept pace with the twentieth.

From his father, Lord Randolph Churchill, he inherited a belief in "Tory Democracy," a conviction that the Conservative position must be revised and rejuvenated. But unlike his father, who died a brilliant failure, young Churchill took the logical consequences of that position; instead of trying to reform the Conservative party from within, he left its ranks, predicting that, like the Republican party in America at the time, it would become increasingly "rigid, materialist, and secular" and it would "cause the lobbies to be crowded with the touts of protected industries." He plainly saw greater political opportunity in the Liberal party. Besides, as the *Times* was to say of him, "Wherever he is, there is his party."

At the outset, his case against the Conservatives was con-servative enough: he championed free trade against protectionism, and economy against government spending. It is ironic today to read the tirades against too large an army budget, delivered by the man who was soon to be a lavishly openhanded First Lord of the Admiralty.

After he crossed the floor of the House and formally became a Liberal, his liberalism became fiercer. "No man has a right to be idle, whoever he be or wherever he lives," said Churchill, and, "We want a government which will think more about the toiler at the bottom of the mine and a little less about the fluctuations of the share market." Later he exclaimed: "The Conservative party is not a party but a conspiracy." He savagely attacked the hampering constitutional role of the House of Lords, to the point where dukes were heard to mutter that they wished they could set their dogs on him. He became something of a political and even a social outcast; the Tories never really forgave him for the defection.

At thirty-three, Churchill was President of the Board of Trade in Asquith's Liberal administration. He had been proposed for the Local Government Board, which included all manner of welfare work, but he said that he refused to be "shut up in a soup kitchen with Mrs. Sidney Webb." Yet, even that great Fabian sybil had to admit that the British welfare state had its beginnings under Churchill. At the Board of Trade he instituted labor exchanges (under William Beveridge, who was later to draft much of postwar Britain's welfare program); he launched unemployment insurance and sickness benefits. However modest their scale, these measures represented a momentous beginning. But Churchill drew a sharp line between liberalism and socialism. "Socialism seeks to pull down wealth; Liberalism seeks to raise up poverty," he said. "Socialism would kill enterprise; Liberalism would rescue enterprise from the trammels of privilege and preference. . . . Socialism exalts the rule; Liberalism exalts the man. Socialism attacks capital; Liberalism attacks monopoly." He declared himself in favor of a greater measure of collectivism, but, he added, "We do not make love collectively, and the ladies do not marry us collectively, and we do not eat collectively, we do not die collectively, and it is not collectively that we face the sorrows and the hopes, the winnings and the losings, of this world of accident and storm."

It is Churchill's attitude toward Communism which perhaps earned him the most rancor in recent times; but it is also through it that he performed his greatest service since the war. He never abandoned the special hostility of the first generation anti-Communist, of the man who saw the Russian Revolution in its full initial savagery, and to whom Communism's international subversion was not, as it is to us, a given and familiar fact but a new and startling outrage. "Of all tyrannies in history, the Bolshevist tyranny is the worst, the most destructive, the most degrading," he said in 1919. "It is sheer humbug to pretend that it is not far worse than German militarism."

As Secretary of State for War after the Armistice, Churchill was in determined charge of the Allied intervention in Russia. Begun as an operation merely to protect Allied supplies and personnel, it continued as a deliberate attempt to prop up the White Russian generals and their armies. They were beyond propping—but it is difficult today to blame Churchill for trying, or for failing to see that, like the French Revolution more than a century before, the Russian Revolution resulted from social upheavals far beyond the reach of military action.

During World War II, as we have seen, Churchill did not hesitate to set aside his anti-Communism in order to make common cause with the Russians against the graver and more immediate menace represented by Hitler. But by 1946, less than a year after the end of the war, he was Cassandra once again, proclaiming the Communist menace to Europe. In his great "iron curtain" speech at Fulton, Missouri, he called on the Western powers, in effect, to form a new defensive alliance against Russia and to seek peace through preponderant strength: "The old doctrine of the balance of power is unsound. We can not afford, if we can help it, to work on narrow margins, offering temptations to a trial of strength." He was, of course, denounced as a warmonger. Yet the Fulton speech soon became part of Western policy, essentially upheld, with some changes in emphasis, by all major political parties ever since.

As the cold war progressed, it was again Churchill who early anticipated the next phase, the phase of wary and qualified "peaceful coexistence." In 1950 he pleaded for "another talk with Soviet Russia upon the highest level," and after his re-election in 1951, he continued to press for a summit. Though he was still widely identified with a hard line on Russia, he rejected the cold-war equivalent of unconditional surrender. "It would, I think, be a mistake to assume," he said, "that nothing can be settled with Soviet Russia unless or until everything is settled." He was no longer in office when "peaceful coexistence" really flourished and the deep divisions in the Communist world opened new possibilities for Western policy, but he had anticipated this, at least in part, when he had pleaded for "a workaday understanding with the Russians."

One of the chief balancing forces weighing against Communism in the postwar era has been the renaissance of western Europe. And one of Britain's greatest problems, as yet unsolved, was caused by the fact that the Empire had gone but the island nation was not yet ready to draw the obvious conclusion and move wholeheartedly into the new Europe. Ironically, it was Winston Churchill, the old imperialist, who was readier than most to turn from the overseas past to the continental present. A few months after he delivered the "iron curtain" speech, he called at Zurich for European unity, and went a long way to suggest Britain's participation in a federated Europe—although he developed doubts about this later. He was a prime mover in the Council of Europe, and he predicted: "There is no doubt that a European Army will be formed as part of the Atlantic Army and I trust that a German contingent will take its place in the European Army on honourable terms." It was not going to be as simple as that, and Churchill had resigned before he could attempt to cope with the organizational intricacies of the Common Market era, or with the new French nationalism that accompanied it. It did not fall to Churchill to lead Britain into the Europe which he had saved. But if any British statesman ever does it, he will have to acknowledge that Winston Churchill pointed the way.

At one point during the Gallipoli crisis, Churchill wrote a letter (never sent) to Foreign Secretary Sir Edward Grey, urging him not to fall "below the level of events." It was a characteristic phrase. From the time a journalist described him enthusiastically as "the youngest man in Europe," very nearly down to the time when, ill and in retirement, he seemed to be the oldest man in Europe, Churchill never fell below the level of events. He made mistakes. He was carried away, not so much by his own oratory, which was always carefully prepared, as by his romanticism and his impatience. He had too much imagination not to act, too much self-confidence not to act on his own. He fought innumerable elections—once he lost three in a row within a matter of two years, only to bounce back in the fourth—and he was a superb parliamentarian in his mastery of the moods and possibilities of the House of Commons. But he was not a good politician, not a clever party man, not a patient compromiser. He knew it and took a certain pride in it. "Everybody threw the blame on me," he said on one occasion. "I have noticed that they nearly always do. I suppose it is because they think I shall be able to bear it best."

In a curious way, his varied life was of one piece, and rarely have we known a career in which the prophecies and accents of youth stayed unashamedly the same into old age. When he was not quite twenty-four a friend predicted that "there will hardly be room for him in Parliament at thirty, or in England at forty." It was true, although he did not become Prime Minister until he had reached an age when other men are ready to retire. In his melodramatic novel, *Savrola,* which Churchill published at twenty-four, he praised "vehement, high, and daring natures"—and that is what he himself remained. Once, recalling his youth, he gave "sincere thanks to the high gods for the gift of existence," and there is no sign that he took it back at any age.

The thanks must be shared by the world. If, as has been suggested above, Winston Churchill was the last great man of the West, the emphasis belongs not so much on the word "great" as on "man" and "West." Other outstanding leaders existed alongside Churchill, though none in his league; others have come to the fore since the height of his career, and still others will appear in the future. Thus it is not the end of greatness that is marked by Churchill's passing, but, in some measure, the end of man—at least as man was able to live, fight, function, and rule, in Churchill's era. And what is also marked by his passing, in some measure, is the end of the West—as the West was able to live, fight, civilize, and govern, in Churchill's era.

He was perhaps the last leader who could still fight a major war on a human and comprehensible scale. As vast and immensely destructive as World War II was, dwarfing as mere provincial scuffles the conflicts of Churchill's youth, its terrible balance sheet could still be written in terms of countable human lives. Though vast fleets of bombers virtually destroyed entire cities, those cities could still fight for survival—at least until Hiroshima. Although each of those bombers was only a minute part of a vast swarm, a sort of infantry of the air, it was still flown by crews with names and identities, skills and qualities, whose individual action and reaction still mattered. And so with the commanders. Although the extent of the fighting, the amount of weapons and supplies, the numbers of men and machines, were immense, they could still be comprehended and controlled by individual leaders looking at a map and reading reports. In short, it was not yet push-button war, automated war, instant war. It was not yet the kind of war in which a leader can only function through a vast network of computers, in which the commander only programs the machine—and in which, one of these days perhaps, the machine will program the commander.

Churchill's was an era when government could still be carried on in a personal style that is becoming increasingly difficult to sustain everywhere; when intuition and amateurish brilliance did not yet have to bow to the relentless specialization and compartmentalization of life. It is difficult to visualize a future First Lord of the Admiralty tinkering with private little experiments to develop a new rocket, as Churchill did with the tank, or a future Prime Minister suggesting the details of a new antimissile device, as Churchill did with his floating harbors for Normandy.

If the meaning of "man" has thus changed since Churchill's heyday, so has the meaning of "West." In one respect, of course, Western civilization has triumphed beyond the hopes or boasts of Kipling's brightest day. Everywhere the technological content of Western civilization, the scientific approach and the industrial method, are desired, admired, and eagerly, if sometimes ineptly, adopted. No religious or political prejudice, no atavism, can any longer hold out against this spread of technology, which is creating what Toynbee called "westernizing" civilizations. But that is not to say that the moral and political content of Western civilization is necessarily spreading too. New powers are gradually moving into the world balance which define themselves neither geographically nor politically as Western. Communism, which is a Western ideology—some have called it a Western heresy—directly attacks the values of the West as Winston Churchill's era knew them and as, indeed, we still know them. If Communism today is more divided and, therefore, perhaps less formidable than it appeared to be when Churchill coined the phrase "iron curtain," it nevertheless remains a challenge of a kind never dreamed of on the North-West Frontier, and still only dimly comprehended at Yalta and Potsdam.

And yet. . .

And yet, who can really believe that "man" and "West" will not endure with something of their old meanings, in the world that Churchill leaves behind? For what man meant to Churchill was really beyond anything the machine can affect; it was the unique gift that human beings have of conquering themselves. What the West meant to Churchill was beyond politics or geography; it was the human desire for freedom, and the courage to bear it. One can, if one is so inclined, regard Churchill as a purely national figure. He will be remembered for everything that is taken to be Anglo-Saxon: courage, pugnacity, humor, love of liberty, and perhaps a certain glorious but insular pride in England. He represented a racial tradition that is at bottom classless: he was baron and yeoman, he was aristocrat and legislator for shopkeepers, he was knight and (despite the knighthood) forever *Mister* Churchill. He had a romantic reverence, scarcely to be found in today's world, for the throne and scepter of England.

But one can also regard him as outside his nation, outside his race, as an exemplar of that moral courage which is as scarce, and as desperately needed, in the age of rockets as it was in the age of cavalry. In a sense beyond the confines of regions or continents, he was a man, and he was of the West.

The Free-lance Warrior Moves into Action

Peace and the British Empire seemed destined to last forever when Lieutenant Winston Churchill sailed with the 4th Queen's Own Hussars to India in 1896. For a cavalry officer pampered by turbaned butlers and dressing boys, "it was," said Churchill, "a gay and lordly life." The regiment, he recalled, had only one serious purpose—polo. Restless to distinguish himself, Churchill added one more: a fierce desire to see action wherever he could find it. As a free-lance warrior with influential family connections, he was able to spend one leave battling Pathan tribesmen on India's North-West Frontier. Then, in 1898, with the Prime Minister's help, he reached the Sudan in time for the celebrated Battle of Omdurman. There, in the African desert, mounted on a polo pony, pistol in hand, Churchill rode with the 21st Lancers against 3,000 Dervish warriors. It was to be the last great cavalry charge in history. Eight months later, Churchill left the army for richer fields.

As a subaltern, above, Churchill wears the full-dress regalia of the 4th Queen's Own Hussars. At right, he sits—out of uniform—among his squadron football teammates.

Churchill, in battle dress, sternly
straddles one of his cavalry ponies (left).
"I was pretty well trained," he said,
"to sit and manage a horse." Below,
British Lancers, depicted in an 1898
painting, clash with fierce Dervishes
at Omdurman. Churchill rode with the
21st Lancers in the cavalry charge.

Churchill (at right, above, as a prisoner) escaped from the Boers soon after his capture. The notice at the right promises a reward for his recapture.

The Escape into Fame

At the age of twenty-five, Churchill set the pattern for his future career. From the misfortunes of war, he would pluck a triumph. In 1899, it was a small war and his triumph was more the stuff of boys' adventure books than of history. An ex-soldier with a living to make, Churchill had set off as a correspondent to cover the Boer rebellion. Two weeks after reaching Capetown, he fell into the hands of the enemy. That was the misfortune; he was carted off to a Boer prison camp. One month later, restless and wretched, Churchill carried out a dangerously modest escape plan. The prisoners knew that a portion of the prison wall was out of sight of the sentries. One night, Churchill clambered over it, straightened his hat, and walked right by the last guard. He now had 300 miles of enemy territory to cross, with the humiliated Boer government in angry pursuit. Traveling in freight trains by night and hiding by day, Churchill reached British territory after two weeks and found himself hero of the hour. Hungry for good news to relay to the home front, the British press had blazoned the tale of the one plucky Englishman who could outwit the Boers. Dignitaries pumped his hand; crowds lined the streets to cheer him. Six months later, while the band was still playing "See, the Conquering Hero Comes!" Churchill ran for Parliament and won. The spotlight never again left him.

Under the banner headline above, Churchill recounts the harrowing story of his escape from the Boer prison for readers of Pearson's Illustrated War News. *Tumultuous crowds hail the young hero, at left, as he steps ashore at Durban after his long trek to freedom.*

As a war correspondent, opposite, Churchill covered the Boer rebellion in South Africa in 1899.

A Brief Pause for Private Matters

Churchill and his fiancée pose for a photograph made in 1908.

Churchill threw himself into politics so furiously that, until he was thirty-three, he had little time for romance. In the glittering social set of his mother, he seemed a confirmed, self-sufficient bachelor. Then Churchill met and quickly married twenty-three-year-old Clementine Hozier, a keen-witted society beauty. It was, said the press, "the political wedding of the year." To Churchill, however, Clementine offered the antidote to politics, a home life that remained serene and revivifying through a half-century of public battles. In the concluding paragraph of *My Early Life*, Churchill himself succinctly summed up his marriage: "Events were soon to arise," he wrote, recalling his battles over the tariff, ". . . which were to . . . absorb my thoughts and energies at least until September, 1908, when I married and lived happily ever afterwards."

With his best man, Lord Hugh Cecil, Churchill arrives (left) at St. Margaret's in Westminster for his wedding on September 12, 1908. Opposite, now the head of his own household, and the head of the Churchill family, Winston joins his mother on a summer afternoon in 1912 at an exhibition in Earl's Court commemorating the Armada.

The Rising Radical Aristocrat

As the President of the Board of Trade, at left, Churchill drives past the Manchester Reform Club in 1909—turning briefly to smile at a hostile group of suffragettes. Opposite, Churchill, then Home Secretary, strides to Parliament in 1910 with his radical ally, David Lloyd George. Below, Churchill tries golf at Cannes. Unable to master that game, he quickly dropped it.

"Winston is the cleverest of all the young men," a Conservative leader once remarked as he surveyed Churchill's dashing apprentice years in politics. As a very junior M.P., Churchill had bemused party elders by taking up his father's battered ensign of "Tory Democracy." Their bemusement turned to anger when he deserted the party for the Liberal opposition. While former colleagues denounced him as "a traitor to his class," Churchill, heedless as always, joined the spellbinding David Lloyd George as a scourge of the landed aristocracy. It was a strange alliance: the poor Welshman and the kinsman of countless peers, who admired each other's genius and shared a streak of the adventurer. At heart, however, Churchill's instincts were conservative, and real radicals like the suffragettes fought him bitterly. A journalist of the day voiced the sentiments of many when he wrote: "Winston follows politics as he would the hounds." No sport compared with it.

A soldier at heart, Churchill, in his regimental uniform, follows British Army maneuvers at right with his wife in 1910. Below, he greets the Kaiser, who had invited him to watch German Army maneuvers.

A Temperament Suited to Crisis

Exhilarated by danger and always ready for combat, the soldier in Churchill always loomed behind the frock-coated civilian leader. In peacetime, Churchill's pugnacity could verge on the comic, as it did in 1911 when, as Home Secretary, he stood amid flying bullets to help police trap a gang of anarchists. The next day in the House of Commons, his political enemies loudly demanded to know why a Cabinet minister risked his life to catch thugs. To many, "The Siege of Sidney Street," as it was called, gave one more proof that Churchill was too reckless to be trusted.

The teapot tempest had barely died down when, a few months later, a real danger at last offered Churchill a field for his energies. Imperial Germany, growing ever more powerful, had laid down a challenge to the powers of Europe. "In such grave and delicate conjunctions," Churchill wrote in *The World Crisis,* "one violent move by any party would rupture and derange the restraints upon all, and plunge Cosmos into Chaos." Overnight, the Home Secretary abandoned domestic reform for grand strategy. About Germany he had no illusions. The weak, vain Kaiser and his awesome army he had seen for himself: a German invasion of France was imminent. His spirits soared and his mind teemed with ideas. Bombarded by Churchill's military schemes and bold predictions, the Prime Minister named him First Lord of the Admiralty. Churchill now had the mighty British Navy to command.

In the front lines of a 1911 gun duel between police and armed thugs, at top, Churchill, in high hat, peers down Sidney Street to watch the action. Immediately summoned before a board of inquiry, at bottom, Churchill is called upon to explain why he, a Cabinet minister, was doing police work.

"The Fleet Was Ready"

Dramatically, Churchill charged the Admiralty with his own keen sense of danger. Guided by the brilliant, fanatical Lord Fisher, he rode roughshod over navy professionals. Oil replaced coal; sleek, fast ships were built and mounted with new fifteen-inch guns. When war came and Churchill fell into disgrace, Lord Kitchener was able to console him: "There is one thing at any rate they cannot take from you: the Fleet was ready."

To aid him in revamping the British Navy,
Churchill, as First Lord of the Admiralty,
brought from retirement the veteran
sea dog Lord Fisher (at left with Churchill).
In 1914 their accomplishment was displayed
in the imposing test mobilization
above. Two weeks later, war broke out.

Mustering New Weapons for War

Churchill, remarked Lloyd George in 1912, "[is] getting more and more absorbed in boilers." As First Lord of the Admiralty, the man who could lament over "chemists in spectacles" ruining the romance of war had become a far-seeing enthusiast of modern technology. The airplane and the tank, perhaps because they were closest to cavalry and especially suited for offensive tactics, delighted Churchill. At his first sight of trenches, he asked engineers to build him an armored car that could smash right over them. When they produced a weird contraption on a caterpillar tread, Churchill ordered twelve of them. They were the first tanks in history—and they belonged to the navy.

British tanks, above, roll to the front in 1918. Developed at Churchill's urging, they were mocked as "Winston's folly."

A flying buff, Churchill completes a seaplane trip, above, before the war.

In a rickety seaplane, Churchill surveys the fleet, above, in 1914. A flier himself, Churchill founded the naval air arm.

Disaster at Gallipoli

When the world war broke out, Churchill was one of the three most powerful men in Britain. Fifteen months later he was a political ruin. The cause—in a word—was Gallipoli. Disaster was born, as Churchill's greatest triumphs were, in a superb strategic concept: a vast outflanking maneuver through the enemy-held Dardanelles strait. With army support denied, the British and French fleets went in alone to capture the prize. Narrowly, they failed. Then disaster struck even harder. Belatedly, the army heeded Churchill's strategy by sending in its own ill-planned expedition to the Dardanelles. On the beaches of Gallipoli, there were over 200,000 casualties. A mountain of bitter recriminations fell upon Churchill. He had staked his reputation on the strategy and he lost. In soul-shattering disgrace he left the government. It was the blackest moment of his life, and it cast a long shadow.

Allied forces crowd a fatally narrow Gallipoli beach at left. In London, below, Churchill broods over the 1915 disaster.

Return to the Circles of Power

The disgrace of the Gallipoli failure—most of it attaching to Churchill—drove him from the circles of power. As restless and self-confident as ever, he turned instead to the front lines, as a battalion commander in France. A few sodden trenches on a quiet front made a severely diminished domain, but Churchill remained cheerfully bellicose. "War," he announced on first taking command, "is declared . . . on the lice." For twenty months it was almost the only war Churchill was called upon to fight. Until Lloyd George became Prime Minister, no politician dared bring Winston back into government. Lloyd George dared: he named Churchill Minister of Munitions. Quickly, war production surged upward as Churchill streamlined the sprawling department and spurred the nation's factory workers. By the time the war ended, his work had won him the U.S. Distinguished Service Medal and a second chance to sit among the leaders.

Navy chief turned combat soldier, Major Churchill visits with a ranking French general in 1915, at left. Above, back in government as Minister of Munitions, Churchill attempts to boost the morale—and output—of factory workers, at lunchtime in 1918.

At a wartime conference, above, Churchill stands behind the French Munitions Minister Loucheur, seated at left, Prime Minister Lloyd George, and Bernard Baruch, Chairman of the American War Industries Board. At left, Churchill accompanies U.S. General Pershing on his parade through London at war's end.

A Postwar Bog of Sums

Churchill leaves his campaign headquarters, above, during an unsuccessful parliamentary contest in 1924.

The Victorian Age was destroyed in the war, and the novel force of a new era slowly began cutting Winston Churchill adrift. The great Liberal party—the political arm of Victorian enlightenment—was dead, its place taken by the harsher, more radical Labor party. Churchill's career—already checkered—took another sharp veer: he attempted to form a new center party around himself and Lloyd George. The attempt failed, and Churchill was left without a party. In 1922, the workingmen of Dundee, who had cheered the aristocratic foe of aristocracy, turned Churchill out of Parliament—for the first time since the century began. Churchill, they saw, was growing deeply conservative. The specter of socialism had come to haunt his imagination and dominate his oratory.

In 1924 he turned back to the Conservatives like a prodigal son. The party that had hounded him for so long offered Churchill the fatted calf: the post of Chancellor of the Exchequer. There, one short step from the prime ministry, Churchill found himself mired in his old, hated bog of sums. His five years as director of the economy marked the only period of Churchill's public life that could be termed ordinary. Economics never commanded his interest, and he once—revealingly—suggested that Parliament hand economic affairs over to experts. Unfortunately, Parliament's business in those days was business.

In 1926 Churchill is feted at a student "rag" (top) in Belfast, Northern Ireland. As Chancellor of the Exchequer, above, he strolls to Parliament on Budget Day in 1929. Back at his desk, below, the director of the economy puzzles over his sums.

51

A Man in His Prime

During the 1920's Churchill was in the robust prime of life. His compact, chubby frame, strong enough at fifty to charge around a polo field, gave him a capacity for work that left his colleagues gasping. He was free, too, of pressing financial worries. A large inheritance from a great-grandmother, the Marchioness of Londonderry, had relieved him for the first time of the burden of writing for a living. In the House of Commons, he had become the acknowledged master of debate, the flamboyant lion of the front benches. Above all, he was a national celebrity whose every move had the public eye. Indeed, the Conservatives had called him into their government largely because he seemed too dangerous to keep outside. Within, he was still a troublesome figure. Stanley Baldwin, the Prime Minister, once complained that Churchill disrupted the work of the Cabinet. "Invariably," he said, "it had to deal with some extremely clever memorandum submitted by him on the work of some department other than his own." He did not care for the intrusions; he could not ignore their cleverness. The party had no great love for the lion in its midst.

In Egypt in 1921 Churchill heads a camel-riding party, above, that includes Mrs. Churchill (left), the explorer Gertrude Bell, and, next to Miss Bell, Churchill's adviser at the 1921 Cairo conference, T. E. Lawrence—the famous Lawrence of Arabia. At right, he warms up after a brisk swim at Deauville with the Duke of Sutherland.

An avid polo player until he was past fifty, Churchill, at left, canters ahead of his friend Prince Edward in 1924. When, as king, Edward was asked to abdicate in 1936, Churchill was virtually his only important supporter. Below, Churchill—Bristol University's new chancellor—keeps his cigar as students carry him through the streets in 1929.

A Return to Private Life

Beginning in 1930, Churchill was out of office for nine years, out of joint with the sickly times, and facing political oblivion. His gifts seemed doomed to erode in idleness. Yet, in the inviolate serenity of his private life, he kept in training, he said, to face "the new young giants" of Parliament. At his country estate he pursued a sane regimen of play, which consisted for Churchill of productive work as remote as possible from politics. As he later wrote of the early thirties, "I never had a dull or idle moment . . . and with my happy family around me dwelt at peace within my habitation." He little knew what menacing giant he would soon be called upon to face, but, scrupulous about his rest and his diversions, he kept himself fit.

Out of the Conservative "Shadow Cabinet" during the 1930's, Churchill remained an active parliamentary gadfly. Above, with his wife and daughter Diana, he wages a victorious campaign in Epping in 1931. Back at his Chartwell retreat, he relaxes with Diana and his son, Randolph, below, and, in an earlier picture at right, with his daughter Mary.

In semiretirement, Churchill walks through the garden where he and his wife spent many leisure hours.

A Lifelong "Joy Ride in a Paint-box"

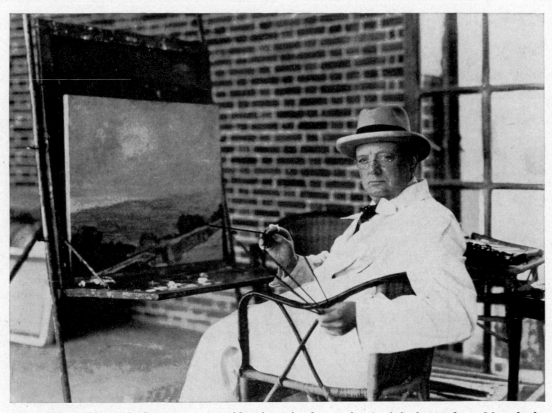

Churchill, at his easel above, was an avid painter in the 1930's. At right he works at Marrakesh.

Above all other hobbies, Churchill loved to paint—wherever he traveled and whenever he could. Painting, he once wrote, urging his pastime on everyone, is ". . . a wonderful new world of thought and craft . . . a mobile and perennial pleasure apparatus." He himself had discovered painting—was "rescued" by it, he said—in the dark days of Gallipoli when he felt "like a sea-beast fished up from the depths. . . ." He fondly recalled his first timid encounter with an empty canvas. He had wished to paint a blue sky. Gingerly, he took the smallest brush and painted a single daub "as big as a bean." Just then, a woman painter who was visiting him rushed impatiently up and, with his largest brush, began hurling "slashes of blue on the absolutely cowering canvas." The spell of the canvas was broken. ("Anyone could see that it could not hit back.") The first quality for an amateur painter, he decided, was "audacity." For fifty more years, Churchill filled hundreds of canvases with bright, decisive landscapes, until his studio was covered from floor to ceiling and the plump figure before the easel became the world's most recognizable Sunday painter.

OVERLEAF: *Churchill's studio at Chartwell is crowded with the output of his pastime.*

Chartwell's Writer in Residence

The grounds of Chartwell provided
landscape for several of Churchill's
best canvases. At right he strolls
by one of the ponds on the estate;
his painting of the Goldfish Pool,
above, was first shown in 1948.

Chartwell, Churchill's quiet and commodious estate outside London, became a bustling work center and playground during the period Churchill was out of political power. Throughout the thirties it was the source of a ceaseless flow of books: *My Early Life, Great Contemporaries, Thoughts and Adventures, Step by Step,* the fifth volume of *The World Crisis* (and a revised one-volume edition of the whole work), and four volumes of *Marlborough: His Life and Times.* To keep busy, Churchill turned his hand to painting, too, and for the sheer fun of it, built part of two cottages and a swimming pool.

Churchill bought Chartwell, above, in 1922. At left, he trowels cement on a brick wall. Never content to be an amateur, even in his hobbies, he joined the Amalgamated Union of Building Trades Workers in 1928.

61

Life Emulates Art

During the 1930's, as Nazi Germany became more menacing, life began to emulate the subject of Churchill's art. From 1931 to 1938 he was intensely absorbed in a grand, self-imposed task: to retell in a final, definitive form the heroic life of the first Duke of Marlborough. In four volumes, written with his own vast knowledge of the way men struggle for power, Churchill described the career of the man who saved England—and half of Europe—from the expanding power of Louis XIV of France. The more he delved into the life of his ancestor, the clearer became the sinister parallel between the past and the present. There, prefigured in family history, was the greedy continental menace, the groping toward a grand alliance, and the need for an unfaltering leader. Churchill's passion to relive that history overflowed onto the canvas at right, which he painted in 1933—the year Hitler came to power. In reproducing the tapestries at Blenheim, Churchill repossessed for himself the buoyant occasion they depict: Marlborough's great victory which crushed the forces of France. While the rest of England vainly dreamed of peace, Churchill was prepared in spirit for the weighty task ahead. Out of power as he was, Churchill had made his pastime a mustering form of action.

Churchill's study at Chartwell,
below, held such mementos
as the portrait of his father
working on a paper (behind
the desk). At right, Churchill
scans a source at his work table.

THE
WRITTEN WORD

Selections from the works of Sir Winston S. Churchill

FIRST MEMORIES

When does one first begin to remember? When do the waving lights and shadows of dawning consciousness cast their print upon the mind of a child? My earliest memories are Ireland. . . .

I have clear and vivid impressions of some events. I remember my grandfather, the Viceroy, unveiling the Lord Gough statue in 1878. A great black crowd, scarlet soldiers on horseback, strings pulling away a brown shiny sheet, the old Duke, the formidable grandpapa, talking loudly to the crowd. I recall even a phrase he used: "and with a withering volley he shattered the enemy's line." I quite understood that he was speaking about war and fighting and that a "volley" meant what the black-coated soldiers . . . used to do with loud bangs so often in the Phoenix Park where I was taken for my morning walks. This, I think, is my first coherent memory . . .

—My Early Life, *1930*

THE SPECTER OF EDUCATION

We continued to toil every day, not only at letters but at words, and also at what was much worse, figures. Letters after all had only got to be known, and when they stood together in a certain way one recognised their formation and that it meant a certain sound or word which one uttered when pressed sufficiently. But the figures were tied into all sorts of tangles and did things to one another which it was extremely difficult to forecast with complete accuracy. You had to say what they did each time they were tied up together, and the Governess apparently attached enormous importance to the answer being exact. If it was not right, it was wrong. It was not any use being "nearly right." In some cases these figures got into debt with one another: you had to borrow one or carry one, and afterwards you had to pay back the one you had borrowed. These complications cast a steadily gathering shadow over my daily life. They took one away from all the interesting things one wanted to do in the nursery or in the garden. They made increasing inroads upon one's leisure. One could hardly get time to do any of the things one wanted to do. . . .

I had a feeling once about Mathematics, that I saw it all—Depth beyond depth was revealed to me—the Byss and the Abyss. I saw, as one might see the transit of Venus—or even the Lord Mayor's Show—a quantity passing through infinity and changing its sign from plus to minus. I saw exactly how it happened and why the tergiversation was inevitable . . . But it was after dinner and I let it go!

—My Early Life, *1930*

THE HERITAGE OF LORD RANDOLPH

All my dreams of comradeship with him, of entering Parliament at his side and in his support, were ended. There remained for me only to pursue his aims and vindicate his memory.

—My Early Life, *1930*

ECHOES OF ANOTHER ERA

[Marlborough's] toils could only be for England, for that kind of law the English called freedom, for the Protestant religion, and always in the background for that figure, half mystic symbol and the rest cherished friend, the Queen.

—Marlborough: His Life and Times, *1934, 1935*

THE ENGLISH SENTENCE—A NOBLE THING

By being so long in the lowest form I gained an immense advantage over the cleverer boys. They all went on to learn Latin and Greek and splendid things like that. But I was taught English. We were considered such dunces that we could learn only English. . . .

As I remained in the Third Fourth three times as long as anyone else, I had three times as much of it. I learned it thoroughly. Thus I got into my bones the essential structure of the ordinary British sentence—which is a noble thing.

—My Early Life, *1930*

WITH THE ARMY IN EGYPT

Every morning in the remote nothingness there appeared a black speck growing larger and clearer, until with a whistle and a welcome clatter . . . the "material" train arrived. . . . At noon came another speck, developing in a similar manner into a supply train. . . . [with] the letters, newspapers, sausages, jam, whisky, soda-water, and cigarettes which enable the Briton to conquer the world without discomfort.

—The River War, *1899*

DECLINE AND FALL OF THE VICTORIAN AGE

This was the British Antonine Age. Those who were its children could not understand why it had not begun earlier or why it should ever stop.

—Pall Mall, *November, 1929*

EARLY CONCLUSIONS, I

It is better to be making the news than taking it; to be an actor rather than a critic.

—The Story of the Malakand Field Force, *1898*

EARLY CONCLUSIONS, II

Chakdara was saved. . . . A thrill of exultation convulsed everyone. In that moment the general, who watched the triumphant issue of his plans, must have experienced as fine an emotion as is given to man on earth.

—The Story of the Malakand Field Force, *1898*

EARLY CONCLUSIONS, III

Far more important than the pleasing baubles of honour is the substantial gift of power.

—The River War, *1899*

THE GREAT WAR

The Great War differed from all ancient wars in the immense power of the combatants and their fearful agencies of destruction, and from all modern wars in the utter ruthlessness with which it was fought. All the horrors of all the ages were brought together. . . . Germany having let Hell loose kept well in the van of terror; but she was followed step by step by the desperate and ultimately avenging nations she had assailed. Every outrage against humanity or international law was repaid by reprisals often on a greater scale and of longer duration. . . . When all was over, Torture and Cannibalism were the only two expedients that the civilised, scientific, Christian States had been able to deny themselves: and these were of doubtful utility.

But nothing daunted the valiant heart of man. Son of the Stone Age, vanquisher of nature with all her trials and monsters, he met the awful and self-inflicted agony with new reserves of fortitude. Freed in the main by his intelligence from mediaeval fears, he marched to death with sombre dignity. His nervous system was found in the twentieth century capable of enduring physical and moral stresses before which the simpler natures of primeval times would have collapsed. Again and again to the hideous bombardment, again and again from the hospital to the front, again and again to the hungry submarines, he strode unflinching. And withal, as an individual, preserved through these torments the glories of a reasonable and compassionate mind.

—The World Crisis, *1923*

AN IDLE THOUGHT

Might not a bomb no bigger than an orange be found to possess a secret power to destroy a whole block of buildings—nay, to concentrate the force of a thousand tons of cordite and blast a township at a stroke? Could not explosives even of the existing type be guided automatically in flying machines by wireless or other rays, without a human pilot, in ceaseless procession upon a hostile city, arsenal, camp, or dockyard?

—Amid These Storms, *1932*

REFLECTION DURING THE THIRTIES

Politicians rise by toils and struggles; they expect to fall; they hope to rise again.

—Strand, *July, 1931*

ATTACKING THE CANVAS

I cannot pretend to feel impartial about the colours. I rejoice with the brilliant ones, and am genuinely sorry for the poor browns. When I get to heaven I mean to spend a considerable portion of my first million years in painting, and so get to the bottom of the subject. But then I shall require a still gayer palette than I get here below. I expect orange and vermilion will be the darkest, dullest colours upon it, and beyond them . . . a whole range of wonderful new colours which will delight the celestial eye.

—Amid These Storms, *1932*

A FURTHER ASSAULT

I write no word in disparagement of water-colours. But there really is nothing like oils. You have a medium at your disposal which offers real power, if you only can find out how to use it . . . you can correct mistakes much more easily. One sweep of the palette knife "lifts" the blood and tears of a morning from the canvas and enables a fresh start to be made; indeed the canvas is all the better for past impressions. . . . You may strike where you please, beginning if you will with a moderate central arrangement of middle tones, and then hurling in the extremes when the psychological moment comes . . . the pigment itself is such nice stuff to handle (if it does not retaliate). You can build it on layer after layer if you like. You can keep on experimenting. You can change your plan to meet the exigencies of time or weather. And always remember you can scrape it all away.

Just to paint is great fun. The colours are lovely to look at and delicious to squeeze out. Matching them, however crudely, with what you see is fascinating and absolutely absorbing. Try it if you have not done so—before you die.

—Amid These Storms, *1932*

A QUIETER PASTIME

It was great fun writing a book. One lived with it. It became a companion. It built an impalpable crystal sphere around one of interests and ideas. In a sense one felt like a goldfish in a bowl; but in this case the goldfish made his own bowl. This came along everywhere with me. It never got knocked about in travelling, and there was never a moment when agreeable occupation was lacking. Either the glass had to be polished, or the structure extended or contracted, or the walls required strengthening.

—My Early Life, *1930*

THE REALIST

The Sermon on the Mount is the last word in Christian ethics. Everyone respects the Quakers. Still, it is not on these terms that Ministers assume their responsibilities of guiding states. Their duty is first so to deal with other nations as to avoid strife and war and to eschew aggression in all its forms, whether for nationalistic or ideological objects. But . . . there is no merit in putting off a war for a year if, when it comes, it is a far worse war or one much harder to win.

—The Gathering Storm, *1948*

A MAXIM TURNED PROPHECY

Real leaders of men do not come forward offering to lead. They show the way, and when it has been found to lead to victory they accept as a matter of course the allegiance of those who have followed.

—Lord Randolph Churchill, *1906*

"MORAL OF THE WORK"

In War: Resolution
In Defeat: Defiance
In Victory: Magnanimity
In Peace: Good Will

—*Motto of the history of* The Second World War

IN WAR: RESOLUTION

Future generations may deem it noteworthy that the supreme question of whether we should fight on alone never found a place upon the War Cabinet agenda. It was taken for granted and as a matter of course by these men of all parties in the State, and we were much too busy to waste time upon such unreal, academic issues.

—Their Finest Hour, *1949*

ADDENDUM

Don't argue the matter. The difficulties will argue for themselves.

—*Memo to the Chief of Combined Operations, 1942*

IN DEFEAT: DEFIANCE

Nothing surpasses 1940. By the end of that year this small and ancient island, with its devoted Commonwealth, Dominions, and attachments under every sky, had proved itself capable of bearing the whole impact and weight of world destiny. We had not flinched or wavered. We had not failed. The soul of the British people and race had proved invincible. The citadel of the Commonwealth and Empire could not be stormed. Alone, but upborne by every generous heartbeat of mankind, we had defied the tyrant in the height of his triumph. . . . Britain, whom so many had counted out, was still in the ring, far stronger than she had ever been, and gathering strength with every day. . . . Hope and within it passion burned anew in the hearts of hundreds of millions of men. The good cause would triumph. Right would not be trampled down. The flag of Freedom, which in this fateful hour was the Union Jack, would still fly in all the winds that blew.

—Their Finest Hour, *1949*

IN VICTORY: MAGNANIMITY

I have always urged fighting wars and other contentions with might and main till overwhelming victory, and then offering the hand of friendship to the vanquished. Thus I have always been against the Pacifists during the quarrel, and against the Jingoes at its close.

—My Early Life, *1930*

IN PEACE: GOOD WILL

My hate had died with [Germany's] surrender.

—Sir Winston Churchill: A Self-Portrait, *1954*

SIDELIGHT: LORD BEAVERBROOK

People who did not know the services he had rendered during his tenure of office or his force, driving power, and judgment as I did, often wondered why his influence with me stood so high. They overlooked our long association in the events of the First World War and its aftermath. Apart from Lord Simon, the Lord Chancellor, with whom, though I greatly respected him, I had never been intimate, Beaverbrook was the only colleague I had who had lived through the shocks and strains of the previous struggle with me. We belonged to an older political generation. Often we had been on different sides in the crises and quarrels of those former days; sometimes we had even been fiercely opposed; yet on the whole a relationship had been maintained which was a . . . warm personal friendship, which had subsisted through all the vicissitudes of the past.

—The Hinge of Fate, *1950*

THE NEW SERVANT

Mankind has never been in this position before. Without having improved appreciably in virtue or enjoying wiser guidance, it has got into its hands for the first time the tools by which it can unfailingly accomplish its own extermination. That is the point in human destinies to which all the glories and toils of men have at last led them. They would do well to pause and ponder upon their new responsibilities. Death stands at attention, obedient, expectant, ready to serve, ready to shear away the peoples *en masse*; ready, if called on, to pulverise, without hope of repair, what is left of civilisation. He awaits only the word of command. He awaits it from a frail, bewildered being, long his victim, now—for one occasion only—his Master.

—The World Crisis, *1929*

AN APPRAISAL . . .

We must regard as deeply blameworthy before history the conduct, not only of the British National and mainly Conservative Government, but of the Labour-Socialist and Liberal Parties, both in and out of office, during this fatal period [of 1931–1935]. Delight in smooth-sounding platitudes, refusal to face unpleasant facts, desire for popularity and electoral success irrespective of the vital interests of the State, genuine love of peace and pathetic belief that love can be its sole foundation, obvious lack of intellectual vigour in both leaders of the British Coalition Government, marked ignorance of Europe and aversion from its problems in Mr. Baldwin, the strong and violent pacifism which at this time dominated the Labour-Socialist Party, the utter devotion of the Liberals to sentiment apart from reality . . . the whole supported by overwhelming majorities in both Houses of Parliament: all these constituted a picture of British fatuity and fecklessness which, though devoid of guile, was not devoid of guilt, and, though free from wickedness or evil design, played a definite part in the unleashing upon the world of horrors and miseries which, even so far as they have unfolded, are already beyond comparison in human experience.

—The Gathering Storm, *1948*

. . . AND A WARNING

There can hardly ever have been a war more easy to prevent than this second Armageddon. . . . Britain, France, and . . . the United States . . . have only to repeat the same well-meaning, short-sighted behaviour towards the new problems which in singular resemblance confront us today to bring about a third convulsion from which none may live to tell the tale.

—The Gathering Storm, *1948*

IN RETROSPECT

I am perhaps the only man who has passed through both the two supreme cataclysms of recorded history in high Cabinet office. . . . These thirty years of action and advocacy comprise and express my life-effort, and I am content to be judged upon them. I have adhered to my rule of never criticising any measure of war or policy after the event unless I had before expressed . . . my opinion or warning about it.

—*Preface to* The Gathering Storm, *1948*

END OF THE GREAT DAYS

It is not so bad as you would expect. Just as eels are supposed to get used to skinning, so politicians get used to being caricatured. In fact, by a strange trait in human nature they even get to like it. If we must confess it, they are quite offended and downcast when the cartoons stop. They wonder what has gone wrong, they wonder what they have done amiss. They fear old age and obsolescence are creeping upon them. They murmur: "We are not mauled and maltreated as we used to be. The great days are ended."

—Amid These Storms, *1932*

EPILOGUE

The span of mortals is short, the end universal; and the tinge of melancholy which accompanies decline and retirement is in itself an anodyne. It is foolish to waste lamentations upon the closing phase of human life. Noble spirits yield themselves willingly to the successively falling shades which carry them to a better world or to oblivion.

—Marlborough: His Life and Times, *1938*

"The Gathering Storm"

Throughout the 1930's, excluded from the circles of power, Churchill "meditated constantly upon the European situation and the rearming of Germany" and tried desperately to alert Britain to the storm he feared was gathering. "To be so entirely convinced and vindicated," Churchill wrote afterward, "in a matter of life and death to one's country, and not to be able to make Parliament and the nation heed the warning, or bow to the proof by taking action, was an experience most painful." Churchill's first warnings came as early as 1932:

Now the demand is that Germany should be allowed to rearm. . . . Do not let His Majesty's Government believe . . . that all that Germany is asking for is equal status. . . . All these bands of sturdy Teutonic youths, marching through the streets and roads of Germany, with the light of desire in their eyes to suffer for their Fatherland, when they have the weapons, believe me they will then ask for the return of lost territories and lost colonies.

—*In the House of Commons, November 23, 1932*

As the thirties wore on, Churchill began to put flesh on his lean prophecies:

[Hitler] had long proclaimed that, if he came into power, he would do two things that no one else could do for Germany but himself. First, he would restore Germany to the height of her power in Europe, and secondly, he would cure the cruel unemployment that afflicted the people. His methods are now apparent. Germany was to recover her place in Europe by rearming, and the Germans were to be largely freed from the curse of unemployment by being set to work on making the armaments. . . . It was not until 1935 that the full terror of this revelation broke upon the careless and imprudent world, and Hitler, casting aside concealment, sprang forward armed to the teeth. . . .

—Strand, *November, 1935*

As his warnings went consistently unheeded, Churchill turned to attack. He delivered this judgment on the Baldwin government in 1936:

So they go on in strange paradox, decided only to be undecided, resolved to be irresolute, adamant for drift, solid for fluidity, all-powerful to be impotent.

—*In the House of Commons, November 12, 1936*

Finally, after Chamberlain agreed to the Munich Pact, Churchill insisted:

We have sustained a total and unmitigated defeat . . . .

And do not suppose that this is the end. This is only the beginning of the reckoning. This is only the first sip, the first foretaste of a bitter cup which will be proffered to us year by year unless by a supreme recovery of moral health and martial vigour, we arise again and take our stand for freedom as in the olden time.

—*In the House of Commons, October 5, 1938*

Overshadowing a prayerful Prime Minister Neville Chamberlain in 1939, Churchill was soon to replace him as Britain's leader.

Beginning of a Holocaust

It was tragically easy during the 1930's to ignore Churchill and his grave, prescient prophecies of danger. While he spoke of the realities of power, his listeners took shelter behind a self-deluding idealism. When he warned of Nazi Germany's re-arming, people retorted that all nations had the right to arm. When he recalled the age-old British policy of maintaining the balance of power, men replied that power politics was the cause of war. Despite Hitler's undisguised ferocity, it was the peaceful Prime Minister who held the nation's confidence. "Peace in our time," Chamberlain assured a grateful people after handing Czechoslovakia to Hitler in 1938. "A total and unmitigated defeat," cried Churchill. It was easier to believe the Prime Minister—until the fateful day in 1939 when the Nazi war machine rolled into Poland and peace in our time lay in ruins. Two days later, England declared war, and the one man in England Hitler had proven to be right was called back to office. At the age of sixty-four, Churchill was once again First Lord of the Admiralty.

WINSTON IS BACK...

At six o'clock that day, Churchill reported for duty. A signal flashed to the ships at sea: "Winston is back." On a Sunday of doubts and crushed illusions, it was the one clear gleam of strength and resolution.

In a vehement speech in 1938, Hitler, above left, makes what he calls his last demand: the German portion of Czechoslovakia. At left, Chamberlain announces "peace with honour" after Munich. Opposite, once again First Lord, Churchill stands on the threshold of Admiralty House—and of a greater calling— the day after Britain declared war.

A Desperate Summons to Command

*An unsmiling Churchill, at top, visits H.M.S.
Exeter after its heroic part in the
destruction of the pocket battleship
Graf Spee. The German ship,
above, burns off Montevideo, where it was
trapped by the navy, December, 1939.*

Incredible as it now seems, England and France still believed, even after declaring war, that no battle with Hitler need be fought. Churchill knew better: men no longer had even the right to seek peace. "We are fighting to save the whole world from the pestilence of Nazi tyranny," he told the House of Commons. "It is a war . . . to establish and revive the stature of man." On land, for eight months, the opposed armies stood idle. At sea, Churchill spurred the navy to strike hard—and it did. In Argentina's River Plate, three British cruisers had trapped the German battleship *Graf Spee*. Off the coast of Norway, a destroyer brazenly rescued 299 British prisoners from a German ship. "In a dark, cold winter," Churchill later reported, the navy "warmed the cockles of the British heart." In the dragging months of halfhearted war, Churchill's determination exhilarated a tense and uncertain people. Then, without warning on the dawn of May 10, 1940, Hitler's Panzer divisions burst into Belgium and Holland, sweeping away with the blitz the half-war, the false hopes, and the half-hearted leaders of England. It left standing, as if limned against the gloom, the one man who spoke in the accent of command. ". . . On the night of the tenth of May, at the outset of this mighty battle," Churchill wrote, "I acquired the chief power in the State . . . At last I had the authority to give directions over the whole scene." That night, while U-boats prowled and the invincible German armies tore through the Low Countries and France, the new Prime Minister went calmly to bed. "I felt as if I were walking with Destiny, and that all my past life had been but a preparation for this hour and for this trial."

Grenade in hand, a German soldier, right, advances with Hitler's blitzkrieg.

New York World-Telegram

7TH SPORTS
Final Stock Tables
Latest Racing on Page 34.

PRICE THREE CENTS

VOL. 72—NO. 266.—IN TWO SECTIONS SECTION ONE

NEW YORK, FRIDAY, MAY 10, 1940.

HOLLAND BATTLES RAGING
NAZIS REPORTED CHECKED
Chamberlain Out, Churchill In

MARINES HEM IN GERMANS   Feel Sympathy   AID RUSHED BY ALLIED TROOPS.

"VERY WELL, ALONE"

The evacuation from Dunkirk, which saved the British Army in June, 1940, is depicted, above, by the English artist Charles Cundall. A British soldier, at left, defiantly alone on a storm-tossed island, was cartoonist David Low's comment on the day Churchill warned the nation that "the Battle of Britain is about to begin."

"It Has Come to Us to Stand Alone"

No Prime Minister ever took office in the face of such onrushing perils. Yet when Churchill first spoke to Parliament as the nation's leader, he seemed to embody all that had turned disasters into triumphs during the nation's long history. "You ask, What is our aim? I can answer in one word: Victory—victory at all costs, victory in spite of all terror, victory, however long and hard the road may be . . . ." Within a month, disaster was mounting to black catastrophe. Incredibly—even to Churchill —a nerveless France was being beaten to a pulp by the swift-moving German tanks. At Dunkirk, over 338,000 troops with their backs to the sea had to be saved from destruction. But when Churchill informed Parliament of that "miracle of deliverance," he warned the nation "not to assign to this deliverance the attributes of a victory." He would not let the nation rejoice in mere safety, for the worst, he knew, was yet to come. Two weeks later it did come: France laid down her arms—conquered in the shocking space of forty days. England was alone. A year before, with the massed French troops at her side, England had feared to do battle with Hitler. Now the troops were gone and Hitler's hardened armies lay just across the Channel. England was fully expected to bid for peace. Hitler expected it, the French expected it, even America's leaders expected it—until they heard Churchill speak to Parliament once more. "The Battle of France is over. . . . the Battle of Britain is about to begin. . . . Let us therefore brace ourselves to our duties, and so bear ourselves that, if the British Empire and its Commonwealth last for a thousand years, men will still say, 'This was their finest hour.'" The British would fight on alone. Their finest hour— and Churchill's—was about to begin.

Just after the fall of France, German troops parade down the Champs Elysées, above, while, below, Hitler does a jig, and Churchill leaves 10 Downing Street for a secret session in Parliament.

"Our Qualities and Deeds Must Burn and Glow"

"The whole fury and might of the enemy," Churchill had warned in June, 1940, "must very soon be turned on us." Weeks later, the bombs of the Luftwaffe began to rain down on Britain's airfields and radar stations—and then on the capital city itself. To destroy the Royal Air Force and break the spirit of Londoners were the Germans' prime aims. They failed at both. Though London was bombed for fifty-seven nights without stop, Churchill reported, "our people are united and resolved as they never have been before." When Churchill visited the ruins to comfort the homeless—as he often did—men called to him in cheerful defiance: "Give it 'em back." Churchill did: he ordered the depleted R.A.F. to bomb Berlin. Englishmen had to be stopped from coming to London from the countryside to share in the dangers. The British had become, as Churchill later wrote, "buoyant and imperturbable"—like Churchill himself. It was no coincidence. The Battle of Britain, for all its terror and anxiety, made Churchill exultant. "We are doing the finest thing in the world," he told Parliament, "and have the honour to be the sole champion of the liberties of all Europe." He saw the battle as he saw all the crises he ever faced: as an opportunity to take one's place in the broad tapestry of Britain's history, and he made ordinary men share his grim joy. As an inspirational leader, this was his greatest gift. He would compare Britain's current trials with fights against tyranny "in the olden time," and the very sound of the archaic words—like those of a schoolboy's history book—touched men's deepest memories. So, long after the blitz was over, Churchill could proudly pay his tribute to his fellow Londoners: "Grim and gay, dogged and serviceable, with the confidence of an unconquered people in their bones . . . they took all they got, and could have taken more."

Their faces lit by raging fires, Churchill and his aides, above, tour the ravaged city streets. Below, Londoners, adapting to the terrors of the blitz, find sleep in a subway tube.

Bombed but unbowed in the blitz, St. Paul's Cathedral looms over London, opposite.

"We shall fight on the beaches," promised Churchill.

"We shall fight on the landing grounds . . ."

"We Shall Go On to the End"

"We shall fight in the fields . . ."

While the bombs fell, Britain and Churchill prepared for the expected invasion. "We shall fight on the beaches," he had promised in his great speech after Dunkirk, and throughout the summer of 1940 Churchill set the nation to work digging in. Tirelessly, he took charge of the vast, hurried preparations for defense of an island that had not, he said, "seen the fires of a foreign camp" for almost a thousand years. Living for long stretches in a special train, he shuttled across the one thousand miles of invadable coast, inspecting and directing the fast-rising fortifications. He formed a home guard of more than a million civilians, armed with shotguns and pikes to defend against enemy parachutists. His orders streamed out inexhaustibly, and usually with a postscript demanding action on the same day. Within weeks, pacific England had become, said Churchill, like a bristling "hornet's nest." There were even men, he recalled later, who looked forward to an invasion for the chance to destroy Hitler's army and its aura of invincibility. But the invasion never came. In October Hitler called off the attack. The Battle of Britain was over.

"And in the streets . . . We shall never surrender . . . ."

A weeping Churchill, standing in the ruins of the House of Commons, vowed to rebuild the chamber "exactly as it was."

Forging "the Grand Alliance"

For a year Churchill himself led Britain's lone stand against the victorious Axis. Then in June, 1941, Hitler invaded Russia, and six months later Japan attacked Pearl Harbor. The Big Three were now in the field, and Churchill took up his most extraordinary role of the war. With Roosevelt confined to a wheel chair and Stalin sphinxlike in the Kremlin, Churchill became the wandering envoy of "the Grand Alliance." At a moment's notice he would travel anywhere to cajole, inspire, and patch up the bitter quarrels. With Roosevelt, Churchill's friendship was warm and close from the day they met off Newfoundland to write the Atlantic Charter and sing "Onward, Christian Soldiers" together. Stalin, on the other hand, was no Christian soldier. A man, Churchill later said, with "a complete absence of illusions of any kind," Stalin was not to be courted. He had to be withstood, and it was Churchill who bore his savage taunts and calculated reproaches. On one memorable occasion in the Kremlin, Churchill hurled back at Stalin all his own pent-up fury. Suddenly, the tension broke. Stalin knew he had met his match. Churchill was "brought up in the House of Commons," he later explained; he did not mind harsh words. But he often kept Stalin's harshness a secret from Roosevelt.

On shipboard off Newfoundland, Churchill and Roosevelt pause in their historic Atlantic Charter conference in 1941, at top, to sing hymns. "It was," said Churchill, "a great hour to live." At left, he salutes an American ship as the conference comes to a close.

Churchill creates a furor among news photographers, above, by appearing in the White House garden in his famed one-piece "siren suit." At right, Churchill meets, for the first time, with Stalin at the Kremlin in 1942. As British seamen cheer, Churchill disembarks at Staten Island, below, during one of his four wartime trips to America.

Mapping
the Attack

In Algiers in 1943,
Churchill eagerly examines
the final plans for the
long-sought invasion of
Italy. He is surrounded
by (from left to right)
Anthony Eden, British
Foreign Secretary; General
Sir Alan Brooke, Churchill's
chief adviser; Air Chief
Marshal Tedder; Admiral
Sir Andrew Cunningham;
and Generals Alexander,
Marshall, Eisenhower,
and Montgomery. While
returning from this
meeting, Churchill learned
that Germans had just
shot down a commercial
plane because spies had
seen it boarded by a
thickset man with a cigar.

Churchill speaks at Albert Hall, at a reunion on the anniversary of the Battle of Alamein.

THE
SPOKEN WORD

Selections from the speeches of Sir Winston S. Churchill

THE YOUNG PARLIAMENTARIAN

[In] war with any great Power . . . three army corps would scarcely serve as a vanguard. If we are hated, they will not make us loved. If we are in danger, they will not make us safe. They are enough to irritate; they are not enough to overawe. Yet, while they cannot make us invulnerable, they may very likely make us venturesome.

—In the House of Commons, May 12, 1901

DEVELOPING A STYLE

They are a class of Right Honourable Gentlemen—all good men, all honest men—who are ready to make great sacrifices for their opinions, but they have no opinions. They are ready to die for the truth, if only they knew what the truth was.

—In the House of Commons, August 14, 1903

EMBELLISHMENTS

[Lord Charles Beresford] can best be described as one of those orators who, before they get up, do not know what they are going to say; when they are speaking, do not know what they are saying; and, when they have sat down, do not know what they have said.

—After appointment to the Admiralty, 1911

OBJECTION SUSTAINED

I remember it was the fashion in the Army when a court martial was being held and the prisoner was brought in that he should be asked if he objected to being tried by the President or to any of those officers who composed the court martial. On one occasion a prisoner was so insubordinate as to answer: "I object to the whole —— lot of you." That is clearly illustrative of the kind of reception which, at this stage, consultation of the trade unions by the Government would meet with.

—In the House of Commons, February 9, 1927

CORRECTING HISTORY

We have all heard of how Dr. Guillotine was executed by the instrument he invented . . . .

[A Right Honourable gentleman: "He was not."]

Well, he ought to have been.

—In the House of Commons, April 29, 1931

APPRAISAL OF A FELLOW M.P.

We know that he has, more than any other man, the gift of compressing the largest amount of words into the smallest amount of thought.

—In the House of Commons, March 23, 1933

A FREQUENTLY BROKEN VOW

All the years that I have been in the House of Commons I have always said to myself one thing: "Do not interrupt," and I have never been able to keep to that resolution.

—In the House of Commons, July 10, 1935

KEY TO RUSSIA

I cannot forecast to you the action of Russia. It is a riddle wrapped in a mystery inside an enigma: but perhaps there is a key . . . Russian national interest.

—A world broadcast, October 1, 1939

THE BEGINNING OF THE UNFORGETTABLE SPEECHES

Come then: let us to the task, to the battle, to the toil—each to our part, each to our station. Fill the armies, rule the air, pour out the munitions, strangle the U-boats, sweep the mines, plough the land, build the ships, guard the streets, succour the wounded, uplift the downcast, and honour the brave. Let us go forward together in all parts of the Empire, in all parts of the island. There is not a week, nor a day, nor an hour to lose.

—At the Free Trade Hall, Manchester, January 27, 1940

TAKING UP THE TASK

I would say to the House, as I said to those who have joined this Government: "I have nothing to offer but blood, toil, tears, and sweat."

We have before us an ordeal of the most grievous kind. We have before us many, many long months of struggle and of suffering. You ask what is our policy? I will say: It is to wage war, by sea, land, and air, with all our might and with all our strength that God can give us: to wage war against a monstrous tyranny, never surpassed in the dark, lamentable catalogue of human crime. That is our policy. You ask, What is our aim? I can answer in one word: Victory—victory at all costs, victory in spite of all terror, victory, however long and hard the road may be; for without victory, there is no survival. Let that be realized; no survival for the British Empire; no survival for all that the British Empire has stood for, no survival for the urge and impulse of the ages, that mankind will move forward towards its goal. But I take up my task with buoyancy and hope. I feel sure that our cause will not be suffered to fail among men.

In the House of Commons, May 13, 1940

RALLYING CRY

This is one of the most awe-striking periods in the long history of France and Britain. It is also beyond doubt the most sublime. Side by side, unaided except by their kith and kin in the great Dominions and by the wide Empires which rest beneath their shield—side by side, the British and French peoples have advanced to rescue not only Europe but mankind from the foulest and most soul-destroying tyranny which has ever darkened and stained the pages of history. Behind them—behind us—behind the armies and fleets of Britain and France—gather a group of shattered States and bludgeoned races: the Czechs, the Poles, the Norwegians, the Danes, the Dutch, the Belgians—upon all of whom the long night of barbarism will descend, unbroken even by a star of hope, unless we conquer, as conquer we must; as conquer we shall.

—A world broadcast, May 19, 1940

THE RESOLUTION

We shall not flag or fail. We shall go on to the end, we shall fight in France, we shall fight on the seas and oceans, we shall fight with growing confidence and growing strength in the air, we shall defend our island, whatever the cost may be, we shall fight on the beaches, we shall fight on the landing grounds, we shall fight in the fields and in the streets, we shall fight in the hills; we shall never surrender, and even if, which I do not for a moment believe, this island or a large part of it were subjugated and starving, then our Empire beyond the seas, armed and guarded by the British Fleet, would carry on the struggle, until, in God's good time, the new world, with all its power and might, steps forth to the rescue and the liberation of the old.

—In the House of Commons, June 4, 1940

BATTLE OF BRITAIN

What General Weygand called the Battle of France is over. I expect that the Battle of Britain is about to begin. Upon this battle depends the survival of Christian civilisation. Upon it depends our own British life, and the long continuity of our institutions and our Empire. The whole fury and might of the enemy must very soon be turned on us. Hitler knows that he will have to break us in this island or lose the war. If we can stand up to him, all Europe may be free and the life of the world may move forward into broad, sunlit uplands. But if we fail, then the whole world, including the United States, including all that we have known and cared for, will sink into the abyss of a new dark age made more sinister, and perhaps more protracted, by the lights of perverted science. Let us therefore brace ourselves to our duties, and so bear ourselves that, if the British Empire and its Commonwealth last for a thousand years, men will still say, "This was their finest hour."

—In the House of Commons (and broadcast), June 18, 1940

CITY OF REFUGE

And now it has come to us to stand alone in the breach, and face the worst that the tyrant's might and enmity can do. . . .

We are fighting *by* ourselves alone; but we are not fighting *for* ourselves alone. Here in this strong City of Refuge which enshrines the title-deeds of human progress and is of deep consequence to Christian civilisation; here, girt about by the seas and oceans where the Navy reigns; shielded from above by the prowess and devotion of our airmen—we await undismayed the impending assault. Perhaps it will come tonight. Perhaps it will come next week. Perhaps it will never come. We must show ourselves equally capable of meeting a sudden violent shock, or what is perhaps a harder test, a prolonged vigil. But be the ordeal sharp or long, or both, we shall seek no terms, we shall tolerate no parley; we may show mercy—we shall ask for none.

—A world broadcast, July 14, 1940

TRIBUTE TO THE AIRMEN

Never in the field of human conflict was so much owed by so many to so few.

—In the House of Commons, August 20, 1940

RESPONSE TO ROOSEVELT

The other day, President Roosevelt gave his opponent in the late Presidential Election a letter of introduction to me, and in it he wrote out a verse, in his own handwriting, from Longfellow which, he said, "applies to you people as it does to us." Here is the verse:

> *. . . Sail on, O Ship of State!*
> *Sail on, O Union, strong and great!*
> *Humanity with all its fears,*
> *With all the hopes of future years,*
> *Is hanging breathless on thy fate!*

What is the answer that I shall give, in your name, to this great man, the thrice-chosen head of a nation of 130,000,000? Here is the answer which I will give to President Roosevelt: Put your confidence in us. Give us your faith and your blessing, and, under Providence, all will be well.

We shall not fail or falter; we shall not weaken or tire. Neither the sudden shock of battle, nor the long-drawn trials of vigilance and exertion will wear us down. Give us the tools, and we will finish the job.

—A world broadcast, February 9, 1941

SIGNOR MUSSOLINI

This whipped jackal, Mussolini, who to save his own skin has made all Italy a vassal state of Hitler's Empire, comes frisking up at the side of the German tiger with yelpings not only of appetite—that can be understood—but even of triumph. . . . this absurd impostor. . . .

—A world broadcast, April 27, 1941

HOW AN ANTI-COMMUNIST CAN SUPPORT THE COMMUNISTS

If Hitler invaded Hell, I would make at least a favourable reference to the Devil in the House of Commons.

—Reply in the House of Commons, June, 1941

MOTTO OF AN ALUMNUS

Never give in, never give in, *never, never, never, never*—in nothing, great or small, large or petty—never give in except to convictions of honour and good sense.

—At Harrow School, October 29, 1941

COPING WITH THE CRITICS

There was a custom in ancient China that anyone who wished to criticise the Government had the right to memorialise the Emperor and provided that he followed that up by committing suicide, very great respect was paid to his words, and no ulterior motive was assigned. That seems to me to have been from many points of view, a wise custom, but I certainly would be the last to suggest that it should be made retrospective.

—In the House of Commons, November 12, 1941

A QUESTION OF UNANIMITY

I feel greatly honoured that you should have invited me to enter the United States Senate Chamber and address the representatives of both branches of Congress. . . . I cannot help reflecting that if my father had been American and my mother British, instead of the other way round, I might have got here on my own. In that case, this would not have been the first time you would have heard my voice. In that case I should not have needed any invitation, but if I had, it is hardly likely it would have been unanimous. So perhaps things are better as they are.

—In the Senate Chamber, Washington, December 26, 1941

A POLITE REFUSAL

I am invited under the threats of unpopularity to victimise the Chancellor of the Duchy [Mr. Duff Cooper] and throw him to the wolves. I say to those who make this amiable suggestion . . . "I much regret that I am unable to gratify your wishes," or words to that effect.

—In the House of Commons, January, 1942

ECHOES OF ST. CRISPIN'S DAY

Some day, when children ask "What did you do to win this inheritance for us, and to make our name so respected among men?" one will say: "I was a fighter pilot"; another will say: "I was in the Submarine Service"; another: "I marched with the Eighth Army"; a fourth will say: "None of you could have lived without the convoys and the merchant seamen"; and you in your turn will say, with equal pride and with equal right: "We cut the coal."

—To owners and miners in coal industry, October 31, 1942

GIVING IT BACK

The Germans have received back again that measure of fire and steel which they have so often meted out to others. . . .

Now this is not the end. It is not even the beginning of the end. But it is, perhaps, the end of the beginning.

—At the Lord Mayor's Day luncheon, Mansion House, November 10, 1942

ASIDE

I am certainly not one of those who need to be prodded. In fact, if anything, I am a prod.

—In the House of Commons, November 11, 1942

THE END IN SIGHT

When Herr Hitler escaped his bomb on July 20 he described his survival as providential; I think that from a purely military point of view we can all agree with him, for certainly it would be most unfortunate if the Allies were to be deprived, in the closing phases of the struggle, of that form of warlike genius by which Corporal Schicklgruber has so notably contributed to our victory.

—In the House of Commons, September 28, 1944

VICTORY

A quarter of a century ago . . . the House, when it heard . . . the armistice terms . . . did not feel inclined for debate or business, but desired to offer thanks to Almighty God, to the Great Power which seems to shape and design the fortunes of nations and the destiny of man; and I therefore . . . move "That the House do now attend at the Church of St. Margaret, Westminster, to give humble and reverent thanks to Almighty God for our deliverance from the threat of German domination." This is the identical motion which was moved in former times.

—In the House of Commons, May 8, 1945

AFTER THE WAR: A NEW STRUGGLE

The Dark Ages may return—the Stone Age may return on the gleaming wings of science; and what might now shower immeasurable material blessings upon mankind may even bring about its total destruction. Beware, I say! Time may be short. . . .

From Stettin, in the Baltic, to Trieste, in the Adriatic, an iron curtain has descended across the Continent. Behind that line lie all the capitals of the ancient States of Central and Eastern Europe—Warsaw, Berlin, Prague, Vienna, Budapest, Belgrade, Bucharest, and Sofia. All these famous cities and the populations around them lie in the Soviet sphere, and all are subject in one form or another not only to Soviet influence, but to a very high and increasing measure of control from Moscow. Athens alone, with its immortal glories, is free to decide its future at an election under British, American, and French observation.

—At Fulton, Missouri, March 5, 1946

HINDSIGHT—AND FORESIGHT

For my part, I consider that it will be found much better by all parties to leave the past to history, especially as I propose to write that history myself.

—In the House of Commons, January 23, 1948

ANOTHER BATTLE

I hope you have all mastered the official Socialist jargon which our masters, as they call themselves, wish us to learn. You must not use the word "poor"; they are described as the "lower income group." When it comes to a question of freezing a workman's wages the Chancellor of the Exchequer speaks of "arresting increases in personal income." The idea is that formerly income taxpayers used to be the well-to-do, and that therefore it will be popular and safe to hit at them. Sir Stafford Cripps does not like to mention the word "wages," but that is what he means. There is a lovely one about houses and homes. They are in future to be called "accommodation units." I don't know how we are to sing our old song "Home Sweet Home." "Accommodation Unit, Sweet Accommodation Unit, there's no place like our Accommodation Unit."

—At Cardiff, February 8, 1950

IN PRAISE OF APPEASEMENT

Appeasement in itself may be good or bad according to the circumstances. Appeasement from weakness and fear is alike futile and fatal. Appeasement from strength is magnanimous and noble, and might be the surest and perhaps the only path to world peace.

—In the House of Commons, December 14, 1950

ON THE RECOGNITION OF RED CHINA

If you recognise anyone, it does not mean that you like him. We all, for instance, recognise the Right Honourable Gentleman [Aneurin Bevan], the Member for Ebbw Vale.

—In the House of Commons, July 1, 1952

THE BRITISH PLAN

In our island, by trial and error and by perseverance across the centuries, we have found out a very good plan. Here it is: The Queen can do no wrong. Bad advisers can be changed as often as the people like to use their rights for that purpose. A great battle is won; crowds cheer the Queen. What goes wrong is carted away with the politicians responsible. What goes right is laid on the altar of our united Commonwealth and Empire.

—At Westminster Hall, May 27, 1953

EPITAPH

I am ready to meet my Maker. Whether my Maker is prepared for the great ordeal of meeting me is another matter.

—Comment, November 30, 1949

Churchill As Strategist

From the time Churchill entered Sandhurst as a young man, problems of strategy and tactics captured his keenest interest. When called upon to lead his country in World War II, he energetically exercised an undaunted command of military affairs —from the most awesome grand strategies to the most minute details of their realization. He was able to write Roosevelt, with equanimity, on the opening of the second front:

Broadly speaking, our agreed programme is a crescendo of activity on the Continent, starting with an ever-increasing air offensive both by night and day and more frequent and large-scale raids, in which United States troops will take part.

—*Letter of April 17, 1942*

In 1944, Churchill broadened his strategic concepts:

At the present stage of the war in Europe our overall strategic concept should be the engagement of the enemy on the largest scale with the greatest violence and continuity. In this way only shall we bring about an early collapse.

—*Note of June 28, 1944*

He buttressed such grandiose schemes by bearing down on details:

Let me have on one sheet of paper a statement about the tanks. How many have we got with the Army? How many of each kind are being made each month? How many are there with the manufacturers? . . . What are the plans for heavier tanks?

—*Memo to Professor Frederick Lindemann, May 24, 1940*

Churchill's insistence upon a taut ship was all-pervasive:

What is the meaning of the expression "Failed to silence machine-gun posts"? It seems an odd description of an action. . . . Surely the way to silence machine-gun posts is to bring up some guns and shell them.

—*Memo to Chief of Imperial General Staff, March 5, 1942*

Churchill's memos contained a barrage of intricate technical questions—how many pounds of armor are used on a certain ship, how many men does it take to clean a boiler, what is the weight of projectiles fired by German tanks—and a request to join a battalion for a day to see its operations. Then, too, he never neglected what he considered the paramount matter of morale.

A serious appeal was made to me by General Alexander for more beer for the troops in Italy. The Americans are said to have four bottles a week, and the British rarely get one. You should make an immediate effort, and come to me for support in case other departments are involved. Let me have a plan, with time schedule, for this beer.

—*Memo to Secretary of State for War, October 23, 1944*

Against his generals' advice, Churchill often visited the front. Above, on the battlefield in France in 1944, Churchill follows with a pointer as one of his commanders describes the enemy's position near Caen. General Montgomery stands at the right.

Commanding the Commanders

As general in chief of all the generals, Churchill had direct control of all the fighting forces of Britain. With the military service chiefs as his advisers, Churchill was a trial and an inspiration to the generals he bullied, charmed, exhausted, and led. In the early hours of the morning, with sleepy-eyed officers as his captive audience, he would stalk the floors pouring out a stream of bold projects for striking at the enemy. Supremely daring himself, Churchill despised caution and orthodoxy in his generals and let them know it in hundreds of scorching cables and stormy interviews that ranged from grand strategy to the smallest details. (He once told the First Lord of the Admiralty that it was a waste of signalmen's and clerks' valuable time to spell out the entire name of the ship *Admiral von Tirpitz* in every cable: "Surely *Tirpitz* is good enough for the beast.") Often he blundered, yet when his highest advisers still feared a German invasion of Britain, Churchill audaciously threw the home reserves into the desert campaign in North Africa—the campaign that eventually turned the tide of war.

Churchill's underground bedroom, above, adjoined the quarters of the war Cabinet in London; the War Room below provided a nerve center for operations. A painting by John Berry, at right, captures part of the North African action.

Unflinching
in Defeat

For two years after Churchill took command, Britain sustained an unbroken series of defeats. Soon after Churchill himself had sent the prize battleship *Prince of Wales* to Singapore, it was sunk by the Japanese. Two months later, he reported worse news: Singapore itself, the great naval fortress, had fallen to land troops. It was, Churchill later wrote, "the worst disaster and largest capitulation in British history . . . the possibility of Singapore having no landward defences no more entered into my mind than that of a battleship being launched without a bottom." Despite such setbacks, Churchill never lost faith in his powers to win victory. As one general noted with awe, he never even lost his appetite. Disaster only made him call more vehemently for new ways to attack, and by the end of 1942, Churchill's plans had begun to bear fruit.

After Pearl Harbor Churchill says good-by (below) to his daughter Mary, before he sails to America. A Japanese painting, at right, records the sinking of the Prince of Wales *and the* Repulse.

Foretaste of Victory

Victory was in sight when D-Day arrived, and Churchill, as always, wanted to be at the front. When General Eisenhower tried to stop him from sailing with the invasion fleet, Churchill said he would evade the ban by joining a ship's company. Only when King George threatened to sail too, did Churchill reluctantly consent to forgo the "refreshment of adventure."

Landing craft and cargo ships poise, above, for the invasion of France, in a painting by Richard Eurich. At left, Churchill crosses the Channel four days after D-Day to look for himself at British forces in Normandy.

"Closing the Ring"

Among the three great Allied leaders, feelings of pride and friendship were never stronger than at Yalta in February of 1945. While four million Allied troops poised for a final smash into enemy territory, the victors-to-be sat down to map out the brave new postwar world, restore just boundaries, and set up a world organization for peace. The conference was punctuated with triumphant toasts among the leaders—Stalin proposed Churchill as "the most courageous of all Prime Ministers in the world." Roosevelt playfully confessed to the mortified Soviet premier that he and Churchill had been calling him "Uncle Joe" throughout the war. Yet despite the good fellowship, Churchill found himself fighting—and in vain—for the rights of small nations that lay in the Red Army's path. His position at Yalta was delicate: in terms of troops in the field, leadership had passed by now from Britain to Russia and America. To be too independent, he told an aide, would be futile. At a small summit dinner party, though, he revealed the somber cast of his thoughts. If a permanent peace were not secured, he warned his two allies, it would be a tragedy for which history never would forgive them.

Crossing the Rhine, above, the day after troops had established a bridgehead, Churchill leads an outing on enemy soil that includes a riverside lunch, at left. Opposite, the three Allied chiefs meet together for the last time, at Yalta in February, 1945. Behind them are (from left to right) Anthony Eden, Edward R. Stettinius, Jr., Sir Alexander Cadogan, V. M. Molotov, and Averell Harriman.

105

At Buckingham Palace on V-E Day, Churchill acknowledges the cheers of the crowd with (from left to right) Princess Elizabeth, Queen Elizabeth, King George VI, and Princess Margaret.

"We May Allow Ourselves a...Period of Rejoicing"

His car hidden by the crowd, Churchill, above, makes a triumphant V-E Day ride to Parliament. Against a sea of jubilant faces, opposite, Churchill once more signals victory. V-E Day, he recalled, was "the greatest outburst of joy in the history of mankind."

At three o'clock in the afternoon on the eighth of May, 1945—almost five years to the day since he had been made Prime Minister—Churchill gave the signal to celebrate victory in Europe. Over the radio, the voice that had growled defiance all through the war for the first time quavered with emotion. "The 'Cease fire' began yesterday to be sounded all along the front. . . . The German war is therefore at an end. . . . Advance, Britannia. Long live the cause of freedom. God save the King." In Parliament, Churchill choked with tears as he rose to thank a cheering House. Twice that day he appeared before tumultuous crowds to share their delight. "God bless you all," he cried out from a ministry balcony. "This is your victory. In all our long history we have never seen a greater day than this." In reply, the immense throng began to sing "For He's a Jolly Good Fellow"—a plain and homely tribute for the man who had comforted them for so long with the splendid language of another age.

The war was not quite over, but in Britain, peace had already broken out. A general election was held, and Churchill flew in from Potsdam to await results. They were incredible. The beloved Winnie of a thousand wartime anecdotes was swept out of office in a landslide. There was no place in peace, the voters seemed to say, for an old man so supremely adapted for the crises of war. The most brutal blow of Churchill's life, it fell eleven weeks after V-E Day.

As the victor, Churchill tries out a chair, above, from Hitler's Berlin bunker and joins hands, at left, with Truman and Stalin at the Potsdam Conference in July, 1945. A few days later a defeated Prime Minister's possessions are removed (right) from 10 Downing Street.

108

"Faithful But Unfortunate"

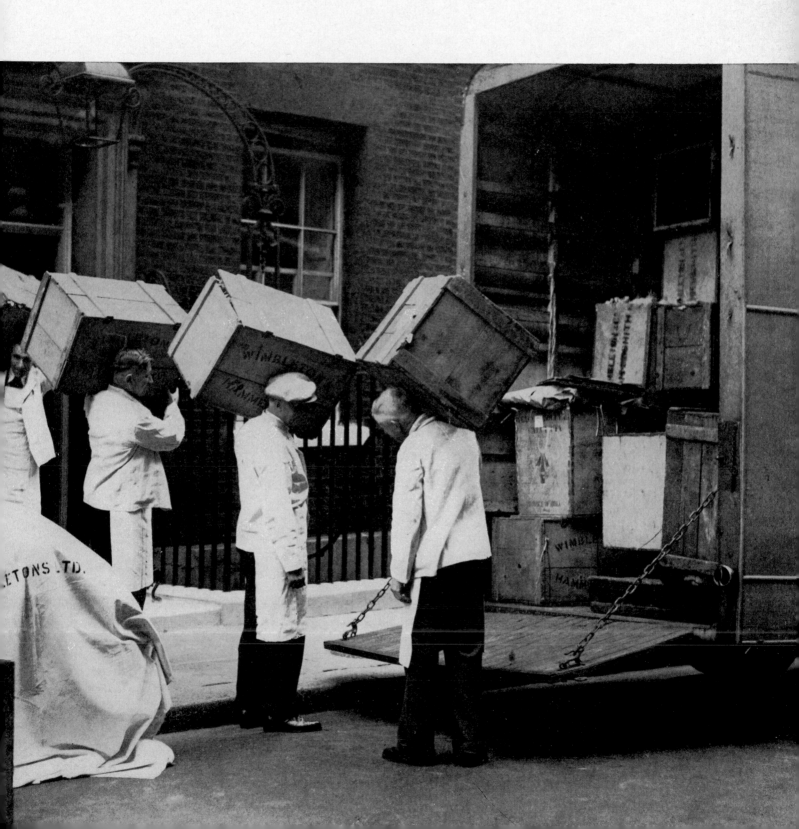

Counselor
of the West

For a few months the election defeat left Churchill stunned and resentful. Bitterly, he refused the King's offer of a knighthood. But the spell did not last. Churchill was too generous to remain bitter and too zestful at seventy to accept his well-wishers' hope that he would retire in all his glory. "I refuse," he announced, "to be exhibited like a prize bull whose chief attraction is its past prowess." Then in March, 1946, he delivered an unpopular fighting speech warning a still-blissful world of the "iron curtain" of Communism. Clearly, Churchill was not yet ready to play the mellow, grand old man.

A standing ovation brings Churchill to tears, above, after his historic call for European unity in 1948. At left, he receives the Croix de la Libération from General de Gaulle in Paris. With his wife and Mrs. Roosevelt, opposite, he visits the late President's grave in 1946. During the same trip, President Truman (opposite, far right), introduces Churchill at Fulton, Missouri, where the prophetic "iron curtain" speech was delivered.

An Unflagging Zest for Life

During the "austerity years" of Labor party rule, Churchill fought idleness and age with his old prescription—hard work in the thick of luxury. From time to time he rose to defend "the historical continuity of our island life" against the Socialists; but he no longer joined the day-to-day battles in the House of Commons. He husbanded his energies, and throughout his seventies they seemed scarcely diminished. During his years out of office, he not only traveled widely as the free world's honored guide and counselor, he managed also to write most of his immense six-volume history of the Second World War. By now his almost invincible constitution had begun to fascinate the world. The *New York Times* once carried the awe-struck headline: CHURCHILL SUFFERING FROM PNEUMONIA: SMOKES TWO CIGARS. He claimed to smoke only fourteen a day; "I like every one of them," he assured a reporter. While there was history left to be made, he defied the nation to lay him to rest. For Churchill there were no honors left to win except that of becoming the architect of a "lasting peace." That, he once said, "is the last prize I seek to win."

Following the hounds at the age of seventy-four, Churchill joins the Old Surrey and Burstow Hunt, above, for a morning outing. At right, Churchill appreciatively pats his horse Colonist II, winner of the Winston Churchill Stakes in 1951. Taking up racing after the war, Churchill had spectacular beginner's luck with Colonist II, who won thirteen races for him. Below, Churchill takes his four-year-old grandson Nicholas Christopher Soames for a stroll in 1952 outside the Westerham Parish Church.

As determined as ever, Churchill concentrates on his dart game, above, at a fair in 1956. At right, with two umbrellas and a policeman to insure privacy, he paints by a lake shore in Italy. Below, convalescing with brandy after a bout of pleurisy, Churchill, at eighty-three, lunches on the Riviera with his wife (back to camera) and his hostess.

Last Call to Office

Finally, at the age of seventy-six, Winston Churchill received the definitive accolade of his extraordinary career: he was called to the nation's highest office in a period of peace. At last, the man for great crises had been acknowledged as a man for all seasons. Churchill's term of office was—it had to be—somewhat anticlimactic. There was no Battle of Britain "about to begin," only the dull and nagging cold war that Churchill set himself to mitigate. Having always enraged progressives by denouncing the Soviet Union, he now irked many Conservatives by calling for coexistence. Once again—even as he approached eighty—Churchill was "ahead of the weather." It seemed at times during his years as Prime Minister, when his wit crackled across the House of Commons, that Churchill would defy time. But not even he could do that.

Above, Churchill greets crowds during the 1951 election in which he was returned to office as Prime Minister. At right, he follows the honor guard in a procession through Windsor Castle courtyard to his installation as a Knight of the Garter in June, 1954.

Churchill attends the annual Harrow festivities at left. In 1954, in his honor, a new verse was added to the old school song "Forty Years On": "Sixty years on—though in time growing older,/ Younger at heart you return to the Hill;/ . . . Long may you fight, Sir, who fearless and eager/ Look back to-day more than sixty years on." Below, Churchill reviews troops as Lord Warden of the Cinque Ports. Opposite, he thanks Parliament for its gift on his eightieth birthday: a portrait done, he conceded, "with force and candour."

The Pride of Men and Nations

"I am now nearing the end of my journey," Churchill informed the members of Parliament on the day of its great birthday celebration for the eighty-year-old Prime Minister. A drum had beat out the "V-for-Victory" symbol in Morse code as he entered the House to receive Parliament's gift: Graham Sutherland's portrait of a withered and formidable old man. Accepting the gift, Churchill had one more dissent to record. Clement Attlee, the Opposition leader, had called him the inspirer of the nation. Churchill disagreed. "It was the nation and the race dwelling round the globe that had the lion's heart. I had the luck to be called upon to give the roar." But not even Churchill could rewrite the account of his finest hours. They no longer belonged to him; they had become the carefully preserved possessions of the nation and of the free world. Some generals in their newly published war memoirs had complained of Churchill's domineering leadership, but by now that only added luster to the record. Churchill was almost beyond criticism—as he was beyond adequate praise. "Give the prizes," he had advised on winning the Nobel Prize for Literature in 1953, "to the men who make you proudest of being a member of the human race." Painter, writer, orator, statesman, he fit the description better than any other man. The prizes, medals, and honors accumulated rapidly with the years, until—while Churchill was yet alive—there were no more prizes for the world to give him.

Churchill, with his son, Randolph, and grandson Winston, poses in courtiers' attire after the Queen's Coronation in 1953.

Final Bow of a Faithful Servant

Four months after his eightieth birthday, Churchill stepped down from office and out of public life forever. The long and marvelous sojourn at the center of events had come to an end. Though he took his place on the back benches of the House of Commons, Churchill took no further part in debates. For a time, members still turned to him, watching to see if he would jump into the fray as pugnaciously as ever. But he would not. In benign detachment he was content at last to sit in the great assembly and watch events flow by him. In the late autumn of his life, Churchill had achieved a deep and merited serenity. For the world there was nothing left but to mark the remaining milestones on his epic journey. In 1958 Churchill and his wife celebrated their golden wedding anniversary. In 1959, on re-election to Parliament at the age of eighty-five, he became the senior member of the House of Commons, in which he had sat—with only one break—for nearly sixty years and across the reigns of six sovereigns. He had once written, "I was happy as a child with my toys in my nursery. I have been happier every year since I became a man." On his eighty-seventh birthday, though enfeebled with age, he walked unaided to his seat in Parliament. In reply to the cheers, he stood up very slowly and spoke six words: "I am grateful to you all." It was the last speech he was to make in the House of Commons. The next year he could no longer attend and decided never again to run for election. In the language of Parliament he was "going home." The last link with public events was broken. Yet Churchill lived on, to appear on his birthdays at the window of his house and give the by now heart-rending victory sign. Each year it would come as a shock—and a poignant delight—to be reminded that he was still present. For, in truth, Churchill had already passed into legend.

Bowing low, Churchill, above, greets Queen Elizabeth, who broke protocol to visit him the evening before he retired as Prime Minister, in 1955. Below, the veteran campaigner receives a hug from his wife after retaining a seat in Commons in a 1955 election.

BY

The President of the United States of America

A PROCLAMATION

Whereas

SIR WINSTON CHURCHILL

a son of America though a subject of Britain, has been throughout his life a firm and steadfast friend of the American people and the American nation; and

Whereas he has freely offered his hand and his faith in days of adversity as well as triumph; and

Whereas his bravery, charity and valor, both in war and in peace, have been a flame of inspiration in freedom's darkest hour; and

Whereas his life has shown that no adversary can overcome, and no fear can deter, free men in the defense of their freedom; and

Whereas he has expressed with unsurpassed power and splendor the aspirations of peoples everywhere for dignity and freedom; and

Whereas he has by his art as an historian and his judgment as a statesman made the past the servant of the future,

Now, Therefore, I, John F. Kennedy, President of the United States of America, under the authority contained in an Act of the 88th Congress, do hereby declare Sir Winston Churchill an honorary citizen of the United States of America.

In Witness Whereof, I have hereunto set my hand and caused the Seal of the United States of America to be affixed.

Done at the City of Washington this ninth day of April in the year of our Lord nineteen hundred and sixty-three, and of the Independence of the United States of America the one hundred and eighty-seventh.

BY THE PRESIDENT:

JOHN F. KENNEDY

GEORGE W. BALL
ACTING SECRETARY OF STATE

Churchill was always held in special regard by Americans, and in 1963 that regard was formalized when he was proclaimed (above) a fellow citizen. America's newly adopted son, at right, looks out of his car window on his last trip to Parliament. "I have pursued life," Churchill once said, "not without pleasure." In richness, variety, and nobility, it had been a life without parallel. That alone could provide some measure of comfort for the world's mourners when at last Winston Spencer Churchill— child of another century and the glory of this one—passed out of the world forever.

A Peaceful Death, A Stately Funeral

On January 24, 1965, two months after Churchill's ninetieth birthday, death came to the century's greatest figure. Felled by a stroke, Churchill remained for days in an ever-deepening coma. On the ninth day of public vigil—it was eight o'clock Sunday morning in London—the end came, and "Great Tom," the state bell of St. Paul's Cathedral, pealed in mourning, heralding one of the most magnificent funerals in all British history.

For three days and nights Churchill's body lay in state where kings had lain—in ancient Westminster Hall, adjoining the House of Commons. Lining up for hours in the bitter January cold, more than three hundred thousand people passed the flag-draped coffin in final homage. Then on a windy Saturday morning, the high pomp and drama of the state funeral began to unfold. To the painfully slow beat of muffled drums, a mile-long procession moved forward with the coffin through the hushed streets of London from Westminster to the cathedral. The coffin, with the insignia of the Garter resting on a black pillow, was borne on a gun carriage reserved for royalty and was guided by the Royal Naval Gun Crew. Out ahead went the bands and banners, the trumpeters, and the glittering guardsmen, mounted and plumed. In sorrow, but more in pride, the British were paying their last tribute to the man who had touched them with greatness.

On a crimson dais and draped in the Union Jack, Churchill lies in state at Westminster Hall, begun in 1097 by King William II.

At right, in a burnished coach loaned by the Queen, Lady Churchill and her two daughters ride through London in the procession to St. Paul's Cathedral. At far right, the Queen's protectors, Life Guards in scarlet coats, ride cavalry horses in the majestic parade.

On a massive gun carriage, Churchill's coffin is pulled, and braked, by detachments of sailors. Airmen escorts carry rifles reversed.

Mighty Tribute
of a Proud Nation

For half an hour, the transept of St. Paul's Cathedral was the focal point of the world's attention. There, under the great dome, Winston Churchill's coffin rested while four kings, two queens, and sixteen prime ministers bowed their heads for a simple Anglican burial service. There, three thousand mourners felt for the last time the influence of Churchill, for, punctuating the service, the congregation sang America's resounding "Battle Hymn of the Republic," as Churchill himself had requested. Then, after the service was completed by trumpeters sounding reveille and the last post, all that was mortal of the great leader continued on its last trip to its last resting place.

Opposite, prayers are said at St. Paul's. Honorary pallbearers, above, include the Earl of Avon (Anthony Eden), left, second from bottom; Earl Attlee, bottom right; and Harold Macmillan, top left. Officers, at right, bear Churchill's decorations.

Public Mourning, Private Grief

Above, seventy-nine-year-old Lady Churchill, son Randolph, and grandson Winston Churchill, twenty-three, watch the coffin as it leaves St. Paul's. At right, members of the royal family at the funeral service include Queen Elizabeth, Prince Philip, the Queen Mother, Prince Charles, Princess Margaret, and Lord Snowdon. Opposite, eight tense young Grenadier Guards, who served as pallbearers through most of the day, bear the heavy, lead-lined coffin down the long steps of the cathedral.

In humble homage to Winston Churchill, Queen Elizabeth broke an ancient royal precedent: she attended the funeral of a commoner. But despite the majesty and the pomp, the chief mourners in this, as in any funeral, were the nearest kin. Ashen-faced and erect, Churchill's wife did not leave the coffin throughout the entire long day. When the body of Churchill was put on a special train at Waterloo Station, the family was alone with its grief. The public ceremonial was over. The burial was in private. Winston Churchill, the greatest of public men, chose to be buried in a modest country churchyard close to Blenheim Palace. The tumult and the shouting were now stilled forever.

CHURCHILL
IN THE CHRONICLES

A selection of comments on Sir Winston S. Churchill

AN ENDURING PRECOCITY

In years he is a boy; in temperament he is also a boy; but in intention, in deliberate plan, purpose, adaptation of means to ends he is already a man. . . . Anyone other than he, being a junior subaltern of Hussars, would be a boisterous, simple, full-hearted, empty-headed boy. But Churchill is a man, with ambitions fixed, with the steps towards their attainment clearly defined with a precocious, almost uncanny judgment as to the efficacy of the means to the end.

. . . He may and he may not possess the qualities which make a great general. . . . In any case, they will never be developed, for, if they exist, they are overshadowed by qualities which might make him, almost at will, a great popular leader, a great journalist, or the founder of a great advertising business. . . .

What he will become, who shall say? At the rate he goes there will hardly be room for him in Parliament at thirty or in England at forty. It is a pace that cannot last, yet already he holds a vast lead of his contemporaries.

—*George W. Steevens,*
in "The Youngest Man in Europe," Daily Mail, 1898

AN EARLY RECOLLECTION . . .

Winston was a large schoolboy when I was still in the nursery. He had a disconcerting way of looking at me criti-

cally and saying nothing. He filled me with awe. His playroom contained from one end to the other a plank table on trestles, upon which were thousands of lead soldiers arranged for battle. He organized wars. The lead battalions were manoeuvred into action, peas and pebbles committed great casualties, forts were stormed, cavalry charged, bridges were destroyed—real water-tanks engulfed the advancing foe. Altogether it was a most impressive show, and played with an interest that was no ordinary child game . . . Winston became a very important person in my estimation.

—*Clare Sheridan,*
a cousin

. . . AND AN APPRAISAL

I used to think he was the naughtiest small boy in the world.

—*Vera Moore,*
his dancing teacher when he was eight

THE SCHOOLBOY

If . . . no greater interest was evinced in Winston Churchill . . . when he entered Harrow than is usually taken in small boys, his own reactions to school life did not allow this long to continue. He consistently broke almost every rule made by masters or boys, was quite incorrigible, and had an un-

Flowers cover the grave of Sir Winston Churchill, opposite,
in a rustic churchyard at Bladon, one mile from Blenheim Palace.

limited vocabulary of "backchat" which he produced with dauntless courage on every occasion of remonstrance.

—*Sir Gerald Woods Wollaston,*
schoolmate at Harrow

A PROMISING POLO PLAYER

As I recall, it was at Poona in the late summer of 1896 . . . A group of officers of the Fourth Hussars, then stationed at Bangalore, called on me. I was ill at the time, but my cousin Shamsuddin entertained them and showed them my horses. When he later told me of their visit he said that among the officers none had a keener, more discriminating eye, none was a better judge of a horse, than a young subaltern by the name of Winston Spencer Churchill. My cousin described him as perhaps a little over twenty, eager, irrepressible, and already an enthusiastic, courageous, and promising polo player.

—*The Aga Khan*

HAS HE STAYING POWER?

What of his future? At thirty-four he stands before the country as the most interesting figure in politics, his life a crowded drama of action, his courage high, his vision unclouded, his boats burned. "I love Churchill, and trust him," said one of his colleagues to me. "He has the passion of democracy more than any man I know. But don't forget that the aristocrat is still there—latent and submerged, but there—nevertheless. The occasion may come when the two Churchills will come into sharp conflict, and I should not like to prophesy the result."

Has he staying power? Can one who has devoured life with such feverish haste retain his zest to the end of the feast? How will forty find him?—that fatal forty when the youth of roselight and romance has faded into the light of common day and the horizon of life has shrunk incalculably, and when the flagging spirit no longer answers to the spur of external things, but must find its motive and energy from within, or find them not at all.

That is the question that gives us pause. For with all his rare qualities, Mr. Churchill is the type of "the gentlemen of fortune." He is out for adventure. He follows politics as he would follow the hounds. He has no animus against the fox but he wants to be in "at the kill." It is recorded that, when a fiery headed boy at Harrow, he was asked what profession he thought of taking up, he replied, "The Army, of course, so long as there's fighting to be had. When that's over I shall have a shot at politics"—not so much concerned about who the enemy may be or about the merits of the quarrel as about being in the thick of the fight and having

a good time. With the facility of the Churchill mind he feels the pulse of Liberalism with astonishing sureness and interprets it with extraordinary ability. But the sense of high purpose is not yet apparent through the fierce joy of battle that possesses him. The passion for humanity, the resolve to see justice done though the heavens fall and he be buried in the ruins, the surrender of himself to the cause—these things have yet to come. His eye is less on the fixed stars than on the wayward meteors of the night. And when the exhilaration of youth is gone, and the gallop of high spirits has run its course, it may be that this deficiency of abiding and high-compelling purpose will be a heavy handicap. Then it will be seen how far courage and intellectual address, a mind acutely responsive to noble impulses, and a quick and apprehensive political instinct will carry him in the leadership of men.

—*A. G. Gardiner,*
1908, editor of the London Daily News

MAN AT THE CENTER

How determined he was never to miss a chance of something happening.

—*The Right Honorable L. C. M. S. Amery,*
fellow Harrovian and M.P.

AN INFORMAL VIEW

He is a little, square-headed fellow of no very striking appearance but of wit, intelligence, and originality. In mind and manner he is a strange replica of his father, with all his father's suddenness and assurance, and I should say more than his father's ability. There is just the same *gaminerie* and contempt of the conventional and the same engaging plain-spokenness and readiness to understand. As I listened to him recounting conversations he had had with [Austen] Chamberlain I seemed once more to be listening to Randolph on the subject of Northcote and Salisbury. About Chamberlain he was especially amusing, his attitude being one of mingled contempt and admiration, contempt for the man and admiration for his astuteness and audacity. In Opposition, Winston I expect to see playing precisely his father's game, and I should not be surprised if he had his father's success. He has a power of writing Randolph never had. . . . He interested me immensely.

—*Wilfrid Scawen Blunt,*
poet and traveler

AUNT MAUD AND THE UNDESIRABLE FIANCE

My father-in-law, Lord Carlisle, once happened to call on Miss Stanley—Aunt Maud, as we used to call her—and found her in tears because her ward, Clementine Hozier, had just become engaged to young Mr. Churchill, of whose political ways Aunt Maud did not approve. About a year afterwards the same subject happened to be mentioned, and Aunt Maud said: "Oh, we all like him so much; he is such a good husband."

—*Professor Gilbert Murray*

HIS OWN IDOL

At dinner he talks and talks, and you can hardly tell when he leaves off quoting his one idol, Macaulay, and begins his other, Winston Churchill.

—*George W. Steevens,*
special correspondent for the Daily Mail

THE LOVE OF ACTION

It was said of a French monarch that no one ever lost a kingdom with so much gaiety. Mr. Churchill was as happy facing a Budget deficit as in distributing a surplus.

—*Philip Snowden,*
former Chancellor of the Exchequer, com-
menting on Churchill's chancellorship

IN THE BROAD TAPESTRY OF HISTORY

He is always unconsciously playing a part—an heroic part. And he is himself the most astonished spectator. He sees himself moving through the smoke of battle—triumphant, terrible, his brow clothed with thunder, his legions looking to him for victory, and not looking in vain. He thinks of Napoleon; he thinks of his great ancestor. Thus did they bear themselves; thus in this rugged and awful crisis, will he bear himself. It is not make-believe, it is not insincerity; it is that in this fervid and picturesque imagination there are always great deeds afoot, with himself cast by destiny in the Agamemnon role. Hence that portentous gravity that sits on his youthful shoulders so oddly, those impressive postures and tremendous silences, the body flung wearily in the chair, the head resting gloomily in the hand, the abstracted look, the knitted brow. Hence that tendency to exaggerate a situation which is so characteristic of him—the tendency that sent artillery down to Sidney Street and during the railway strike dispatched the military hither and thither as though Armageddon was upon us. "You've mistaken a coffee-stall row for the social revolution," said one of his colleagues to him as he pored with knitted and portentous brows over a huge map of the country on which he was making his military dispositions.

—*A. G. Gardiner,*
1912, in the London Daily News

PRAISE (SLIGHTLY RESERVED)

Winston has a hard temperament, with the American's capacity for the quick appreciation and rapid execution of new ideas, whilst hardly comprehending the philosophy beneath them. But I rather liked the man. He is under no delusions about himself.

—*Beatrice Webb (Mrs. Sidney Webb),*
prominent Fabian

UNUSUAL AMBITIOUSNESS

His ambition was in essence disinterested. I do not say that he was always wise—but his patriotism burnt with a pure flame throughout. Hard fighter as he is in debate, he is a man devoid almost of rancour. A defeat does not sour him, even though it depresses him, nor does it turn him into a hater of the successful half of political mankind. And he possesses another virtue—exceptionally rare in politics—or, for that matter, almost anywhere. He is strictly honest . . . to other people, down to the smallest details of his life.

—*Lord Beaverbrook,*
newspaper publisher

THE PAINTER

I remember in his early painting days when we were both staying in a country house, set in a monochrome of dull, flat, uneventful country, I went out to watch him paint, half wondering what he would make of it. Looking over his shoulder I saw depicted on his canvas range upon range of mountains, rising dramatically behind the actual foreground. I searched the skies for a mirage and then inquired where they had come from—and he replied: "Well—I couldn't leave it quite as dull as all that." No landscape and no age in which he lived could ever be consigned to dullness. But in his own there was no need to snatch the brush out of the hands of Fate.

—*Lady Violet Bonham Carter,*
long-time leader in Britain's Liberal party,
later Baroness Asquith

FOLLOW THE LEADER

Some men hang themselves on their politics, others hang their politics on themselves, and these need to be stout pegs, well screwed into the scheme of things, as indeed Mr. Churchill is. He manages it very well. His first party will still have no good said of him, his second believes him to be hankering after his first love, and latterly he has been advertising for a new Centre Party which is to combine the charms of the other two. But even if this third match came off and then turned out ill, Mr. Churchill would not be greatly embarrassed, for wherever he is, there is his party.

"Front Bench Figures," The Times, *of London,*
November 15, 1920

OPINION OF AN EARLY MENTOR

I like him. He is one of those challenging personalities whom some people like very much, and some people hate very much. I belong, quite frankly, to the former class. I admire his dazzling mind, his brilliant mind, so brilliant as to dazzle his judgment. In fact, one of his troubles is that his headlights are rather blinding—and he finds it difficult to drive a straight course on the road, and to avoid smashing into traffic.

—*David Lloyd George,*
former Prime Minister, in a speech of May 8, 1925

THE HANDYMAN

He had tiny hands and he used to wear two pairs of gloves. I remember once he was driving a nail into a brick and the head came through the finger of the gloves, pinning them to the wall.

He said, "Tiggy (that's my nickname), look what I've done. How will I get it off?"

"Take your hand out of the gloves," I told him. He laughed and said, "I'm a ruddy fool." When I told him I had not said that, he answered, "No, but you b—— well think so." That's how he was.

—*Harry Whitbread,*
tutor to Churchill in the art of bricklaying

CHURCHILL'S VIEWS . . .

No part of the country smaller than the whole country is Churchill's country. No sectional interest has ever been his special interest. He never commanded the unquestioning party adulation granted to Mr. Whatshisname or Mr. Never Mind. Though he never disinclined to take office, a refusal to compromise in order to get it kept him out of it for eleven years; and if it be objected that he has often changed his party, I would be prepared to argue that the changes have been made only to suit unchanging views.

—*Colin Coote,*
British journalist

. . . AND OTHERS'

Just try the process of outlining to Churchill a view with which he does not agree. You will find restive movements developing into mutterings, mutterings developing into thunderclaps, and thunderclaps finally being followed by a torrential rain of argument in which your poor little view is utterly swamped. He can never resist snatching at any idea which may be floating about, squashing it if he thinks it is a mosquito, and causing it to flutter iridescently if he thinks it a butterfly.

—*Colin Coote*

THE OPPOSING FORCES

It was indeed a happy stroke of fate that against the sheer ranting mob-mastery of Hitler and Mussolini, raving to millions of people who had, for the nonce, sold themselves into intellectual and moral slavery, there should be set a Churchill who could, and did, with richer power of speech, raise his people, touch their spirits to noble issues, and give to every individual a new sense of power and responsibility.

—*R. G. Menzies,*
Prime Minister of Australia

TAKING THE INITIATIVE

When he came back to the Admiralty, at the outbreak of the Second World War, I was at sea: I remember with what excitement the Fleet received the signal: "Winston is back." Now we shall begin to get a move on, everyone said: but it was not until Mr. Churchill became Prime Minister that we really got going.

In the autumn of 1941 it must have seemed to many people in every country difficult to foresee a time when Britain would ever again be able to take the initiative. Not to Mr. Churchill, however: he not only clearly foresaw the time when we should regain the offensive but he was already planning for it!

—*Lord Mountbatten*

"KLOP"

Idiosyncrasies which in more ordinary men are petty and annoying seem in a man of his stature to become acceptable and not a little amusing. He cannot tolerate paper clips of any sort and he simply abominates pins. Any documents which came in by post were always subjected to searching examination, the offending pins, etc., removed and replaced by green tags, of which we always had an assortment of sizes and lengths. A paper punch was used to make holes for these tags and during my very first evening with him he astonished me by looking up from the pages of a letter I had just handed him for signature and saying the one word, "Klop." He was obviously asking me to give him something but I had not the remotest idea what it was. Seeing my bewilderment, he explained that he meant "a paper punch." "When I say 'Klop,' Miss Shearburn, *that* is what I want."

—*Mary Shearburn Thompson,*
former secretary to Churchill

THE WAR CABINET

A Churchill Cabinet was primarily an opportunity for the Prime Minister to tell his colleagues what was happening, what he thought about it, and how he meant to deal with it, followed by as much of the agenda as time allowed. . . . But one could wish that some of Churchill's discourses could have been recorded for the benefit of posterity. Most memorable of these talks was one given to all his colleagues of Cabinet rank at the time of the Dunkirk evacuation, when he told us that we could hardly hope to save more than forty-five thousand men, and, after surveying all the consequences, added that whatever else happened we should, of course, fight on. My mind went back to what was once said of the great Chatham, that no one ever "left his Cabinet without feeling himself a braver man."

—*The Right Honorable L. C. M. S. Amery*

RETURNING TO UNIMPEACHABLE PRECEDENT

Winston never had the slightest doubt that he had inherited all the military genius of his great ancestor, Marlborough. His military plans and ideas varied from the most brilliant conceptions at the one end to the wildest and most dangerous ideas at the other. To wean him away from these wilder plans required superhuman efforts and was never entirely successful in so far as he tended to return to these again and again.

—*General Sir Alan Brooke*
(later Viscount Alanbrooke)

THE VISITING PRIME MINISTER

[During all of Churchill's] visits, my husband worked long hours every day. The Prime Minister took a long nap every afternoon, so was refreshed for hard work in the evening and far into the night. While he was sleeping, Franklin had to catch up on all his regular work. Even after Franklin finally retired, if important dispatches or messages came in, he was wakened no matter what the hour, and nearly every meal he was called on the telephone for some urgent matter. It always took him several days to catch up on sleep after Churchill left.

—*Eleanor Roosevelt*

HOW CAN ONE DISLIKE HIM?

I do my best to dislike Churchill; there is abundant reason why I should; indeed, as one of his political opponents, it is expected of me. His activities during the Labour Government's term of office from 1945 onward I found deplorable; his ideas are to me reactionary, he is out of touch with modern social trends. But he has served his country with the highest distinction; in moments of peril he was undaunted; in majestic phrases, which linger in the memory of those who heard them, he crystallised the resolution of the whole nation. Many blunders occurred in the war for which he must bear the responsibility; to me and to millions of our fellow countrymen his social ideas and activities are anathema. Yet, how can one work up an intense dislike for a man who has "borne the heat and burden of the day," whose abilities are unquestionable, even though directed into the wrong channels, and who concentrates in his person such varied and brilliant qualities?

—*The Right Honorable Emanuel Shinwell,*
Labor party M.P.

THE SECOND CHANCE

To those of us who had the unforgettable experience of working in direct touch with the human dynamo which was Winston, it often seemed that the moving spirit which governed all his actions and thoughts was expressed by the tab so often attached to the head of papers coming down from him—"Action this day."

There were times when it would appear that he would almost prefer action at any cost providing it was immediate.

It was this universal urgency that often led to impatience and sometimes injustice where individuals were concerned, but none of such errors of judgment which history may disclose can for one moment dim the splendour of Winston's finest hour in 1940 when, almost at a word, he inspired the nation to a degree of unity which it had never known before or since, a unity which, under his personal, inspiring leadership, gave our civilisation another chance.

—*Air Chief Marshal Tedder,*
(later Baron Tedder)

TURNED OUT OF OFFICE IN 1945

His nature, identified with a magnificent enterprise, his countenance, etched by the fires and frosts of great events, had become inadequate to the era of mediocrity.

—*Charles de Gaulle,*
President of France

THE DEFEATED PRIME MINISTER

For a while we stood in silence, looking at [his] gaily-coloured painting. Churchill was motionless. He was far away in his own imaginings.

When, presently, he began to speak, it was clear that his

thoughts now flickered to and fro between the portrait and the memory of his defeat.

"Another few days and I shall be proud of it," he said, staring at the picture. "And I shall be able to spend quite a time in painting during these last few years which are left to me. . . . Yes. It needs a little mauving in. . . . But the term of my mandate has been withdrawn by the people. . . .

"Yes. It does need touching up a bit. . . . And certainly leisure will be pleasing. And I am grateful for having been given the chance to rest during the few years left to me. . . . But it will be strange on the morrow when the great affairs of State are no longer brought to me."

Then with an effort he raised his head from the picture and moved slowly towards the door. Each step that he took seemed heavy with pain. At the door he paused.

"But I have no regrets," he said.

For an instant he hesitated. His eyes were bleary with tears. Slowly his gaze wandered round the four of us. But he was heedless of our presence. His mind was far away, ranging perhaps over lobbies and battlefields, assemblies and oceans, palaces and the broken slums of London.

"I have no regrets," he repeated.

"I leave my name to history."

And he walked out of the room.

—Robin Maugham,
author, recalling the day of Churchill's defeat

A MORAL MAGNIFICENCE

It has always seemed to me that Winston Churchill combined within himself—within one man—almost all the qualities which we humans can possess, and as with all humans, they were not by any means all good. Of all his remarkable traits I would put "domination" as the most prominent. He must dominate. . . . Never has any land found any leader who so matched the hour as did Sir Winston Churchill . . . When he spoke—in words that rang and thundered like the Psalms—we all said: "That is how we feel" and "That is how we shall bear ourselves." . . . He gave us the sense of being a dedicated people with a high purpose and an invincible destiny. There was—there is—a moral magnificence about him which transforms the lead of lesser men into gold; he inspired us all . . .

Field Marshal Montgomery

AMERICA'S HONORARY CITIZEN

Whenever and wherever tyranny threatened he has always championed liberty. Facing firmly toward the future he has never forgotten the past. Serving six sovereigns of his native Great Britain, he has served all men's freedom and dignity.

Now his stately ship of life, having weathered the severest storms of a troubled century, is anchored in tranquil waters, proof that courage and faith and zest for freedom are truly indestructible. The record of his triumphant passage will inspire free hearts all over the globe.

—John F. Kennedy,
in his remarks at conferral of Honorary Citizenship on Sir Winston Churchill, April 9, 1963

RESOLUTION IN THE HOUSE OF COMMONS

That this House desires to take this opportunity of marking the forthcoming retirement of the Right Honourable Gentleman the Member for Woodford by putting on record its unbounded admiration and gratitude for his services to Parliament, to the nation, and to the world; remembers above all his inspiration of the British people when they stood alone, and his leadership until victory was won; and offers its grateful thanks to the Right Honourable Gentleman for these outstanding services to this House and to the nation.

—Moved and unanimously passed on the eve of Sir Winston's retirement from the House, July 28, 1964

A LACK OF COMPARISONS

There have been, no doubt, debaters and orators of equal resource and power, but few with that gift of puckish and rather mischievous humour which so endears him to us.

The life of the man whom we are honouring is unique. The oldest among us can recall nothing to compare with him, and the younger ones among us, however long we live, will never see the like again.

—Harold Macmillan,
in the House of Commons, July 28, 1964

THE SUMMATION

It is fairly safe to say that his enduring fame in the world at large and in the eyes of posterity will rest in large measure on the great events of a few years; and all the years that had gone before will be regarded as the years of preparation. He was blessed with length of days, and he came to the supreme achievement of his life schooled and disciplined by long experience of great affairs, familiar with the handling and control of national problems, full of practical wisdom, and with a part to play that he alone could most magnificently fulfil. The "tooth of time and rasure of oblivion" work their inexorable will, and men who bestrode the earth in their day are frequently forgotten as the long years pass by. But Sir Winston Churchill, it may be confidently said, will never be forgotten.

—Lord Justice Birkett

Orders, Decorations,
and Medals of
Sir Winston Spencer Churchill

(a partial list)

Knight Companion of the Most Noble Order
of the Garter
Privy Councilor
Order of Merit
Companion of Honor
Fellow of the Royal Society
Nobel Prize for Literature
Grotius Medal of the Netherlands
Charlemagne Prize
Williamsburg Award
Freedom House Award
Benjamin Franklin Medal
First Class Order of Military Merit of Spain
Punjab Medal
Egyptian Medal with Clasp
Queen's Medal for South Africa
1914–1915 Star
1939–1945 Star
Africa Star
Italy Star
France and Germany Star
Knight Grand Cross of Order of Leopold of Belgium
Knight Grand Cross of Order of Lion
of the Netherlands
Chevalier of Order of Elephant of Denmark
Grand Cross of Order of St. Olav
of Norway, with Chain
Grand Cross of Order of Oak Leaf Crown
of Luxembourg
Order of Star of Nepal
Belgian Croix de Guerre with Palm
French Croix de Guerre with Palm
Danish Liberation Medal
Croix de la Libération
Médaille Militaire of France
United States Distinguished Service Medal
Military Medal of Luxembourg
Lord Rector of Aberdeen University

Rector of Edinburgh University
Chancellor of Bristol University
Honorary Fellow, Merton College, Oxford
Honorary Bencher, Gray's Inn
Companion of Literature
Chairman of the Trustees,
of Churchill College, Cambridge
Honorary Academician Extraordinary
of the Royal Academy
Elder Brother of Trinity House
Lord Warden of the Cinque Ports
Grand Seigneur of Hudson's Bay Company
Sunday "Times" Literary Award and Medal
Liveryman of Mercers' Company
Honorary Life Member of the Association
of Men of Kent and Kentish Men
Honorary Life Member of the Friendship Veterans
Fire Engine Company of Alexandria, Virginia

Honorary citizen of the United States of America; of the states of West Virginia, Tennessee, Hawaii, New Hampshire, Nebraska, North Carolina, and Maryland; and of the cities of Paris, Athens, Marathon, Thebes, Aeglion, Naupactus, Strasbourg, Nancy, Roquebrune-Cap-Martin, Brussels, Antwerp, and Luxembourg.

Honorary freeman of Edinburgh, City of London, Wanstead and Woodford, Aberdeen, Westminster, Blackpool, Birmingham, Beckenham, Stafford, Ayr, Woodstock, Darlington, Brighton, Manchester, Eastbourne, Perth, Aldershot, Cardiff, Kensington, Worcester, Bath, Portsmouth, Sheffield, Deal, Dover, Wimbledon, Aberystwyth, Leeds, Poole, Rochester, Harrow, Belfast, Londonderry, Hastings.

Honorary degrees from the colleges and universities of Oxford, Rochester (U.S.A.), Queen's (Belfast), Bristol, Harvard, McGill, Brussels, Louvain, Miami, Westminster (Fulton, Missouri), Columbia, Aberdeen, Leyden, New York, Oslo, London, St. Andrew's, Liverpool, Cambridge, and Copenhagen.

Chronological Summary of the Life of Sir Winston Churchill

1874
Born Winston Leonard Spencer Churchill at Blenheim Palace, November 30

1888
Enters fourth form at Harrow School

1892
Wins Public Schools' fencing competition

1893
Sent to tutor for help in passing Sandhurst entrance examinations, succeeds on his third attempt

1894
Passes out of Sandhurst, eighth in a class of 150

1895
Father dies, January 24; gazetted to 4th Hussars in March, watches Spanish forces in Cuba, writes for *Daily Graphic*

1896–97
Serves as correspondent with Malakand Field Force on India's North-West Frontier, writes for *Daily Telegraph,* then attached to 31st Punjab Infantry in India

1898
Serves with Kitchener's army in Egypt, joins the charge of the 21st Lancers at the Battle of Omdurman in Sudan, publishes his first book, *The History of the Malakand Field Force,* writes dispatches for *Morning Post*

1899
Returns to India, resigns commission, contests Oldham in parliamentary by-election and loses to Walter Runciman, sets out for Boer War as *Morning Post* correspondent, is taken prisoner, November 15, escapes from Pretoria compound on December 12, publishes *The River War* and his only novel, *Savrola*

1900
Returns to England and is elected Conservative Member of Parliament for Oldham, publishes *London to Ladysmith* and *Ian Hamilton's March*

1901
Makes maiden speech in Parliament, February 18

1904
Crosses floor of House to join Liberal party

1906
Elected Liberal Member for North-West Manchester and is made Under Secretary of State for Colonies, publishes *Lord Randolph Churchill*

1908
President of Board of Trade in Asquith government, is defeated in North-West Manchester by-election, elected Liberal Member for Dundee, publishes *My African Journey,* marries Clementine Hozier, September 12

1909
Birth of first daughter, Diana, July 11. Publishes *The People's Rights*

1910
Re-elected Liberal Member for Dundee, appointed Home Secretary

1911
Appears at "Siege of Sidney Street," becomes First Lord of the Admiralty. Birth of his only son, Randolph, May 28

1914
Mobilizes British Fleet on own initiative. Birth of his second daughter, Sarah, October 7

1915
Forced to leave Admiralty after Gallipoli disaster, appointed Chancellor of Duchy of Lancaster in May, resigns on November 11 to join army in France

1916
Serves with 6th Royal Scots Fusiliers, returns to political life in England

1917
Appointed Minister of Munitions

1918
Re-elected Liberal Member for Dundee and designated to assume post of Secretary of State for War and for Air. Birth of third daughter, Marigold Frances, November 15 (died August 23, 1921)

1921
Appointed Colonial Secretary

1922
Contests general election as National Liberal Member for Dundee and loses. Birth of fourth daughter, Mary, September 15

1923
Contests by-election as National Liberal at Leicester West and loses. First of four volumes of *The World Crisis* is published

1924
Contests by-election at Westminster and loses, is elected Constitutionalist Member for Epping in October general election, becomes Chancellor of Exchequer in Baldwin government, rejoins Conservative party

1926

Edits *British Gazette* (published by government during General Strike)

1928

Joins Amalgamated Union of Building Trades Workers

1929

Elected Member for Epping, becomes Rector of Edinburgh University and Chancellor of Bristol University

1930

Publishes *My Early Life*

1931

Resigns from Conservative "Shadow Cabinet," re-elected Conservative Member for Epping

1932

Publishes *Thoughts and Adventures*

1933

Publishes first of four volumes of *Marlborough: His Life and Times*

1935

Writes article for *Strand* magazine warning against Hitler and German rearmament

1937

Publishes *Great Contemporaries*

1938

Publishes *Arms and the Covenant* (American edition titled *While England Slept*)

1939

Appointed First Lord of the Admiralty in Chamberlain government, September 3

1940

Summoned to post of Prime Minister on May 10, forms Coalition government, speech in House on May 13 ("blood, toil, tears, and sweat"), speech in House on June 4 ("We shall fight on the beaches"), speech in House on June 18 ("This was their finest hour")

1941

Signs Atlantic Charter on August 12 with President Franklin Roosevelt aboard *Prince of Wales,* visits Canada and United States after Japan's entry into war

1942

Signs United Nations Pact on January 1, flies to Cairo in August, gives Montgomery command of Eighth Army, arrives in Moscow, August 12, and meets with Russian Premier Stalin

1943

Confers with Roosevelt in Casablanca in January (where "unconditional surrender" policy is decided upon), attends Cairo and Tehran conferences in November

1944

Visits Normandy beaches on June 10, attends Second Quebec Conference with Roosevelt in September (where Allied zones of occupation in Germany are discussed), meets Stalin in Moscow in October, and sees de Gaulle in liberated Paris in November

1945

Attends Yalta Conference with Roosevelt and Stalin, announces end of European war on May 8, attends Potsdam Conference in July, resigns as Prime Minister after party defeat in general election

1946

Makes speech at Fulton, Missouri, in March (the "iron curtain"), advocates United States of Europe in speech at Zurich in September

1947

Has two paintings accepted by Royal Academy

1948

Publishes *Painting as a Pastime* and first volume of six on *The Second World War*

1949

Wins first horse race in August with Colonist II

1951

Returned to office as Prime Minister on October 26 after Conservative victory in general election

1952

Visits United States, confers with Truman

1953

Invested Knight of the Garter, April 24, awarded Nobel Prize for Literature in October, attends Bermuda Conference in December with Eisenhower and French Prime Minister Laniel

1954

Installed as Knight of the Garter, June 14

1955

Resigns as Prime Minister, April 5

1956

Publishes first two volumes of four on *History of the English–Speaking Peoples*

1963

Declared Honorary Citizen of United States, April 9, announces intention not to stand for re-election to House of Commons

1964

Presented with vote of thanks from House for parliamentary career, July 28

1965

Dies at Hyde Park Gate home, January 24

Order of the Funeral March

Two Bands of: The Royal Air Force
Detachments of: Battle of Britain Aircrews
The Royal Air Force
The 4th/5th (Cinque Ports) Battalion The Royal Sussex Regiment (T.A.)
The 4th Battalion The Essex Regiment (T.A.)
The 299th Field Regiment Royal Artillery (T.A.)
(Royal Buckinghamshire Yeomanry, Queen's Own Oxfordshire Hussars, and Berkshire)
The Honorable Artillery Company (T.A.)
The Royal Military Academy, Sandhurst
Two Bands of: Her Majesty's Foot Guards
Detachments of: The Welsh Guards
The Irish Guards
The Scots Guards
The Coldstream Guards
The Grenadier Guards
Two Bands of: The Royal Marines
Detachments of: The Royal Marine Forces Volunteer Reserve
The Royal Marines
The Royal Naval Reserve
The Royal Navy
A Drum Horse and State Trumpeters of the Household Cavalry
First Detachment of the Household Cavalry
Two Bands of: Her Majesty's Foot Guards

Air Chief Marshal	Admiral	General
Sir Charles Elworthy,	Sir David Luce,	Sir Richard Hull,
Chief of the Air Staff	Chief of Naval Staff	Chief of the General Staff
	and First Sea Lord	

Admiral of the Fleet, the Earl Mountbatten of Burma, Chief of the Defense Staff

Orders and Decorations of the Deceased borne by Officers of
The Queen's Royal Irish Hussars

The Banner of the Cinque Ports
borne alternately by Officers of
The Queen's Royal Irish Hussars

The Banner of Spencer-Churchill
borne alternately by Officers of
The Queen's Royal Irish Hussars

A.D.C. to the General Officer
Commanding London District

Brigade Major of the Household
Brigade

The Chief of Staff London District
Brigadier J. W. Berridge

The General Officer Commanding London District and
Major-General Commanding the Household Brigade
Major-General E. J. B. Nelson
(Commanding Troops on Parade)

The Earl Marshal, The Duke of Norfolk

Royal Naval Gun Crew (Forward Detachment)

Bearer Party of Her
Majesty's Brigade of Guards

Bearer Party of Her
Majesty's Brigade of Guards

Escort of the
Royal Air Force

THE
GUN
CARRIAGE

Escort of the
Royal Air Force

Royal Naval Gun Crew (Rear Detachment)

The Family
and Other Principal Mourners

Second Detachment of the Household Cavalry
Band of the Royal Artillery

Band of the Metropolitan Police

Contingents of: The Police   The Fire Services   The Civil Defense Corps

The Seating Plan in St. Paul's Cathedral

	Trinidad — Mr. Rose	
	Trinidad and Tobago	North Screen
	Jamaica — Min. of Trade	Liechtenstein — Crown Prince
	Tanzania — Min. of Ext. Affairs	Jordan — Prince Hassan
	Sierra Leone	Sweden — Prince Bertil
	Cyprus — Min. of Commerce	Ethiopia — Crown Prince
	Nigeria — Min. of Justice	Zambia — President
	Malaysia — Wife of High Com.	Uruguay — President
	Malaysia — High Com.	Israel — President
	Ghana	Iceland — President
	Ceylon — High Com.	Capt. Abel-Smith (rep. Princess Alice)
	Mrs. Grimond	Prince Michael of Kent
	Mr. Grimond	Angus Ogilvie
	Lady Douglas-Home	Princess Alexandra
	Sir Alec Douglas-Home	Duchess of Kent
	Mrs. Harold Wilson	Duke of Kent
	Mr. Harold Wilson	Princess Marina

West Door

Uganda	France	The Queen
Uganda	France	Duke of Edinburgh
Kenya	U.S.A.	Queen Mother
Malawi	U.S.A.	Prince of Wales
	U.S.A.	Princess Margaret
	U.S.S.R.	Lord Snowdon
	U.S.S.R.	Duke of Gloucester
	United Nations	Duchess of Gloucester
	Canada — P.M. Mr. Lester Pearson	Princess Royal
	Mrs. Lester Pearson	Prince William of Gloucester
	Australia — Lord Casey	Prince Richard of Gloucester
	Lady Casey	Sir John Aird (rep. Duke of Windsor)
	New Zealand — P.M. Mr. Keith Holyoake	
	Malta — P.M. Dr. Borg Olivier	
	Mrs. Borg Olivier	
	India — Mr. Swaran Singh	
	Pakistan	South Transept

Catafalque

Seats for Pall Bearers — King Frederik of Denmark, King Baudouin of Belgium, Queen Juliana of Netherlands, Prince Bernhard of Netherlands, King Olav of Norway, King Constantine of Greece, Grand Duke of Luxembourg, President de Gaulle of France

Lady Churchill, Randolph Churchill, Sarah Churchill, Mary Churchill Soames, Christopher Soames, Winston Churchill II — Seats for Pall Bearers — Earl Marshal Duke of Norfolk

Churchill Family Mourners

Key: 1 The Lord Chancellor's mace   2 The table bearing Churchill's chivalric orders   3 The Speaker's mace   4 Dais flanked by giant candlesticks

Reflections on the Man

THE QUEEN'S MESSAGE TO THE HOUSE OF COMMONS

I know that it will be the wish of all my people that the loss which we have sustained by the death of the Right Honourable Sir Winston Churchill, K.G., should be met in the most fitting manner and that they should have an opportunity of expressing their sorrow at the loss and their veneration of the memory of that outstanding man who in war and peace served his country unfailingly for more than fifty years and in the hours of our greatest danger was the inspiring leader who strengthened and supported us all.

Confident that I can rely upon the support of my faithful Commons and upon their liberality in making suitable provision for the proper discharge of our debt of gratitude and tribute of national sorrow, I have directed that Sir Winston's body shall lie in state in Westminster Hall and that thereafter the funeral service shall be held in the Cathedral Church of St. Paul's.

—Queen Elizabeth II

END OF THE BATTLE

The battle that was joined on January 14, between the irresistible force and the immovable object, has ended.

The infinite patience of death, in its merciless compassion, chipped away at the granite, bit by bit, until the dust was at last ready to return to the dust.

—Bernard Levin

A GOOD HOUSE OF COMMONS MAN

Winston Churchill, and the legend Winston Churchill had become long before his death and which now lives on, are the possession not of England, or Britain, but of the world; not of our time only but of the ages . . .

He brought his own tempestuous qualities to the conduct of our parliamentary life. Where the fighting was hottest he was in it, sparing none—nor asking for quarter. The creature and possession of no one party, he has probably been the target of more concentrated parliamentary invective from, in turn, each of the three major parties than any other member of any parliamentary age, and against each in turn he turned the full force of his own oratory.

If we on this side of the House still quote as a classic words he uttered over half a century ago, about the party he later came to lead, the honourable members opposite have an equally rich treasure house for quotations about us . . .

He was a warrior, and party debate was war, it mattered, and he brought to that war the conquering weapon of words fashioned for their purpose, to wound, never to kill; to influence, never to destroy . . .

For now the noise of hooves thundering across the veldt, the clamour of the hustings in a score of contests, the shots in Sidney Street, the angry guns of Gallipoli, Flanders, Coronel, and the Falkland Islands, the sullen feet of marching men in Tonypandy, the urgent warnings of the Nazi threat, the whine of the sirens, and the dawn bombardment of the Normandy beaches—all these now are silent.

There is a stillness, and in that stillness, echoes and memories . . .

Each one of us recalls some little incident—many of us, as in my own case, a kind action graced with the courtesy of a past generation and going far beyond the normal calls of parliamentary comradeship. Each of us has his own memory, for in the tumultuous diapason of the world's tributes all of us here at least know the epitaph he would have chosen for himself: "He was a good House of Commons man."

—Harold Wilson,
Prime Minister of the United Kingdom

HISTORY'S CHILD

When there was darkness in the world, and hope was low in the hearts of men, a generous Providence gave us Winston Churchill. As long as men tell about that time of terrible danger and of the men who won the victory, the name of Churchill will live. Let us give thanks that we knew him. With our grief let there be gratitude for a life so fully lived, for service so splendid, and for the joy he gave by the joy he took in all he did. . . . He is history's child, and what he said and what he did will never die.

—President Lyndon B. Johnson

ABOVE THE MERELY GREAT

The power and the glory are gone, the soaring oratory, the eloquent pen, the cherubic face, the impish twinkle in his eyes, the jaunty cigar, the vitality that sparked a world.

One measure of Churchill's greatness is that no one today, now that the blaze of his genius has subsided into dust and ashes, need explain or describe or grope for words. He is one of those rare figures in history who stand like sky-scrapers above the merely great. Usually history waits to recognize its supreme leaders, but there is no need to wait in Churchill's case. . . .

A man like Winston Churchill makes everyone a part of his life, as if a little of that greatness were shared by each of us.

—New York Times

THE GREAT DELIVERER

All the world now knows, what only a few in places of high responsibility knew at the time, that his apparently effortless authority over the whole conduct of war was in fact exercised through a daily conflict of wills with his chief professional advisers, who on occasion opposed him not only on tactical detail but on major strategic principle. Whether risks were needlessly taken, whether victory could have been achieved at less cost in blood and treasure, whether a different kind of victory, leaving a better world order than we now enjoy, might by other means than Churchill's have been won—these are questions that cannot yet be finally answered. What cannot be doubted is that the nation's ablest captains of war, the men whom Churchill chose as supreme commanders and staff officers and whose choice the fact of victory and the consensus of their professions have ratified, including the men whose day-to-day differences with the Prime Minister have been most canvassed, were all agreed that they would rather suffer the strain of constant disagreement with their political chief, and see their skilled advice overruled even in matters of strategical life and death, than accept the direction of any other man.

—The Times *of London, an editorial, January 25, 1965*

THE FULL SPLENDOR OF OUR HUMAN ESTATE

Today we meet in sadness to mourn one of the world's greatest citizens. Sir Winston Churchill is dead. The voice that led nations, raised armies, inspired victories, and blew fresh courage into the hearts of men is silenced. We shall hear no longer the remembered eloquence and wit, the old courage and defiance, the robust serenity of indomitable faith. Our world is thus poorer, our political dialogue is diminished, and the sources of public inspiration run more thinly for all of us. There is "a lonesome place against the sky." . . .

So we are right to mourn. Yet, in contemplating the life and spirit of Winston Churchill, regrets for the past seem singularly insufficient. One rather feels a sense of thankfulness and encouragement that throughout so long a life, such a full measure of power, virtuosity, mastery, and zest played over our human scene.

Contemplating this completed career, we feel a sense of enlargement and exhilaration. Like the grandeur and power of the masterpieces of art and music, Churchill's life uplifts our hearts and fills us with fresh revelation of the scale and reach of human achievement. We may be sad; but we rejoice as well, as all must rejoice when they "now praise famous men" and see in their lives the full splendor of our human estate.

He used to say that he was half American and all English. But we put that right when the Congress made him an honorary citizen of his mother's native land and we shall always claim a part of him. I remember once years ago during a long visit at his country house he talked proudly of his American Revolutionary ancestors and happily of his boyhood visits to the United States. As I took my leave I said I was going back to London to speak to the English-Speaking Union and asked if he had any message for them. "Yes," he said, "tell them that you bring greetings from an English-Speaking Union." And I think that perhaps it was to the relations of the United Kingdom and the United States that he made his finest contribution.

—*Ambassador Adlai E. Stevenson, United States Representative to the United Nations, at the Memorial Service for Sir Winston Churchill, National Cathedral, Washington, D.C., January 28, 1965*

WHO IS THERE TO TALK OF?

You know, when I'd help him near the end there, I might grab his hand a little too hard and it would press the ring on his finger and he'd give a little growl and say, "Easy now," and just for a moment you imagined him back running things again. Well, he's gone now. When the King is dead, you say "The King is Dead, Long Live the King." What do you say now? Who is there to talk of?

—*Sergeant Edmund Murray, Scotland Yard (Churchill's bodyguard)*

NEVER ALOOF

Twenty years ago, before the postwar election, the editor of *The Times* decided that his paper should say that Mr. Churchill ought to carry himself in the campaign, not as a partisan, but as the national and world leader that he was; and that, afterwards, he ought not to make the mistake of staying too long on the scene, but should pass at the apt moment into a dignified and fruitful retirement. Being both brave and fair-minded, the editor felt that he must tell the great man beforehand what he proposed to say. Mr. Churchill's retorts to the two propositions were characteristic and illuminating: to the first, the reply was simply, "Mr. Editor, I fight for my corner"; to the second, it was, "Mr. Editor, I leave when the pub closes." This was no elder above the battle—which, as it happened, he lost. It was Churchill.

—The Economist *of London*

THE FULL POTENTIAL

Sir Winston performed many services for mankind but none greater than revealing to all of us the full potential of man.

—Denver Post

A CHERISHED FRIEND

A giant has gone out from among us. We are all the poorer for his going. I have lost a cherished friend. Britain has lost her most luminous son, free men everywhere have lost their champion.

—Bernard Baruch

A HIGH RANK

His services to his fatherland and to the free world will assure him a high rank in world history after his long, strenuous life, richly blessed with success.

—Ludwig Erhard,
Chancellor of West Germany,
in a message to Lady Churchill

IN THE GREAT DRAMA

For everyone in my country as for myself, Sir Winston Churchill is and will remain the one who—in directing the admirable British war effort to victory—contributed powerfully to the well-being of the French people and the liberty of the world. In the great drama he was the greatest.

—President Charles de Gaulle of France

AMONG THE MEMORIALS

We at the United Nations feel a particular grief in the death of one who played such a vital role in the formation of our organization, from its conception in the Atlantic Charter to its realization in San Francisco. This achievement takes its place alongside countless others and together with his inspiring leadership and his own late historical works will always remain as a memorial to him.

—U Thant,
Secretary General of the United Nations,
in a message to Prime Minister Wilson

THERE CAN BE NO LEAVE-TAKING

There can be no leave-taking between him and the people that he served and saved . . . Many of us today may be feeling that by his going the scale of things has dwindled, our stature is diminished, that the glory has departed from us, that "there is nothing left remarkable beneath the visiting moon." I remember yesterday seeing his face for the last time: a face from which all age and infirmity had fallen away —young, calm, resolute in death. And I wondered: "Is there anything, or is there nothing left that we can do for him?" Then I remembered the words of his victory broadcast, when he urged us not to fall back into the rut of inertia and confusion and the craven fear of being great. I knew that that

pattern of greatness which he impressed on the spirit of the nation is what he would ask from us today.

—Baroness Asquith,
(formerly Lady Violet Bonham Carter), in her maiden speech in the House of Lords, January 25, 1965

HE WAS MY FRIEND

Warrior, statesman, orator, writer, painter, he was my friend and I honoured and loved him. He was one of the select of history, who became immortal during his lifetime.

—John Diefenbaker,
Opposition leader, Canadian Parliament

STILL POINT OF THE TURNING WORLD

Now we are at one of the still points of the turning world. The link which stretched back to Queen Victoria and Gladstone has snapped.

Today all freedom-loving men and women claim Sir Winston as their own, and mourn his death, and well they may, because it is in large measure due to him that some of us are free at all. . . .

He certainly enjoyed power, and that was plain to see. But great leader though he was, he was never haughty; he was never remote. He might be overbearing, he might be unfair but never mean or cynical. And he enjoyed also all luxuries which we ourselves would like to enjoy: and this I think is what endeared him to so many people.

They saw in him their ambitions, and indeed their vices writ large. They liked his warmth and his generosity, and the open display he gave of his anger and his pleasure. They liked the pleasure he took in life itself.

—Jo Grimond,
Leader of the Liberal party

A DANGEROUS ADVERSARY

[He was] a great Englishman, one of the greatest of his time, a tower of strength to his own people and to their allies in their hour of need. . . .

We in Ireland had to regard Sir Winston over a long period as a dangerous adversary. The fact that he did not violate our neutrality during the War must always stand to his credit, though he indicated that in certain circumstances he was prepared to do so.

—Eamon de Valera,
President of Ireland

REMEMBERED IN RUSSIA

The tireless efforts of Sir Winston during the war against Hitlerite Germany are remembered in the Soviet Union and the grief of the British people in this bereavement is shared here.

—Alexei N. Kosygin,
Premier of the Soviet Union

ALWAYS LOOKING FOR "FINEST HOURS"

So far as Churchill the historian is concerned, I have always admired his prose much more than his content. It seems to me that somebody would get a curious idea of what has been going on in this country for the last 2,000 years if they had to get it all from Winston. He leaves too much of the important stuff out.

If there was one thing that marked him off from the comparable figures in history, it was his characteristic way of standing back and looking at himself—and his country—as he believed history would. He was always, in effect, asking himself, "How will I look if I do this or that?" And "What must Britain do now so that the verdict of history will be favourable?" All he cared about, in Britain's history . . . were the moments when Britain was great. He was always looking around for "finest hours," and if one was not immediately available, his impulse was to manufacture one. . . .

He was, of course, above all, a supremely fortunate mortal. History set him the job that he was the ideal man to do. I cannot think of anybody in this country who has been favoured in this way so much. Winston was superbly lucky. And perhaps the most warming thing about him was that he never ceased to say so.

—Earl Attlee,
former Labor party leader

THE GREAT BOURGEOIS

Sir Winston Churchill was one of the greatest bourgeois politicians.

—Prague Radio

THE CAPACITY FOR TOTAL RESPONSE

The human potential is the most magical but also most elusive fact of life. . . . Because of Winston Churchill, millions of people discovered their ability to come fully alive. They knew they faced total danger, but he helped them to find their capacity for total response. . . .

Courage to him was more than a spirited charge into a hurricane of flying bullets. It was a wondrous human assortment—hearty laughter, warm feelings, and the enjoyment of living in general. The ability to come fully alive was to be seen not solely in terms of a full adrenalin response to danger but in comprehending the creative possibilities that come with the gift of life. There was nothing freakish about versatility; what was unnatural, rather, was the man who permitted himself to develop only in a single direction. The highest privilege was the freedom to choose; the meanest affliction was to live without option. He gave options to a world quickly running out of time and space.

—Norman Cousins,
in the Saturday Review

MY OLD FRIEND—FAREWELL

Upon the mighty Thames, a great avenue of history, move at this moment to their final resting place the mortal remains of Sir Winston Churchill. He was a great maker of history, but his work done, the record closed, we can almost hear him, with the poet [Tennyson] say:

> Sunset and evening star,
> And one clear call for me! . . .
>
> Twilight and evening bell,
> And after that the dark!
> And may there be no sadness of farewell,
> When I embark; . . .

Winston Churchill was Britain—he was the embodiment of British defiance to threat, her courage in adversity, her calmness in danger, her moderation in success. Among the Allies his name was spoken with respect, admiration, and affection. Although they loved to chuckle at his foibles, they knew he was a stanch friend. They felt his inspirational leadership. They counted him a fighter in their ranks. . . .

With no thought of the length of time he might be permitted on earth, he was concerned only with the quality of the service he could render to his nation and to humanity. Though he had no fear of death, he coveted always the opportunity to continue that service.

At this moment, as our hearts stand at attention, we say our affectionate, though sad, good-by to the leader whom the entire body of free men owes so much. . . .

May God grant that we—and the generations who will remember him—heed the lessons he taught us; in his deeds; in his words; in his life.

May we carry on his work until no nation lies in captivity; no man is denied opportunity for fulfillment.

And now, to you, Sir Winston—my old friend—farewell.

—Dwight D. Eisenhower,
in a broadcast, as Churchill's coffin was carried up the Thames by launch

A NOTE ON THIS BOOK

This book was produced jointly by United Press International and the American Heritage Publishing Company, under the following editorial direction: for UPI, Earl J. Johnson, Editor and Vice President, and Harold Blumenfeld, Executive Newspictures Editor; for American Heritage Publishing Company, Joseph J. Thorndike, Editor-in-Chief, and Richard M. Ketchum, Editor of the Book Division.

Staff for the book was as follows: Editor, Charles L. Mee, Jr.; Art Directors, Elton Robinson and Jack Newman; Picture Editor, Mary Sherman Parsons; Copy Editor, Suzanne Smith; Editorial Assistants, Joan Bunche and Susan Lewis. The text blocks and captions were written by Walter Karp.

All pictures, except as otherwise credited, come from the files of UPI. The Editors are particularly indebted to Anthony Montague Browne, Sir Winston Churchill's secretary, and to Jack Le Vien, producer of the film *The Finest Hours.*

The cover picture was taken the day before V-E Day in the garden of 10 Downing Street. On the back cover: Sir Winston's heraldic arms as Knight of the Garter.

Picture credits: Birnback Publishing Service (Ullstein), 76–77 bottom. Black Star, 79 top, 110 left, 123 all, 125 both, 127. British Travel Association, 22–23. Brown Brothers, 32 left, 34, 36 bottom. Central Press Photos Ltd., 74 bottom. Collection of Sir Winston Churchill, 20, 21, 60 top. European Picture Service, 43 bottom, 45 top, 79 bottom left. Fox Photos, 55. FPG, 50, 51 middle and bottom, 88, 112 top and bottom, 113 top, 114 left, 116 both. © Toni Frissell, 1959, 118. Manchester *Guardian,* 38 top. © Philippe Halsman, 60 bottom. Hills and Saunders, 26 both. *Illustrated London News,* 17, 21, 33 bottom, 42–43 top, back cover. Imperial War Museum, 44, 48 left, 78 top, 82 top and third down, 86–87, 97, 99, 102–103 top, 104–105 all, 107, 108 both. © Karsh, Ottawa—Rapho Guillumette, 6. Jack Le Vien Productions, 33 top, 35 top, 40 bottom, 51 top, 52 left, 56, 58–59, 64 bottom, 84 top, 85 top right, 98

both. © London *Daily Express* from London *Evening Standard,* June 18, 1940, 78 bottom. *Life,* 20, 60 top. Alec Murray, 18 bottom, 24 both color. National Portrait Gallery, 18 both. Pictorial Parade, 32 bottom right, 35 bottom, 57, 74 top, 103 bottom, 113 bottom, 128. Pix (Camera Press), cover, 2. Radio Times Hulton Picture Library, 25 right, 27 right, 36 top, 38 bottom, 41 bottom, 46–47 both, 64 top, 106 top, 110–111 top. Reuter, 37, 39, 40 top, 41 top, 45 bottom, 52 right, 119 top. Brian Seed, 61 top. Collection of Mrs. Christopher Soames, 62–63. London *Sun,* 109. Topix, 54 middle. United States Air Force, 100–101.

The Editors would like to express thanks for permission to quote from the works of Sir Winston Churchill.

Excerpts from *Amid These Storms,* pages 27, 250, 265, 308, 313; *My Early Life: A Roving Commission,* pages 1, 16, 17, 27, 62, 212, 330, 331; Volumes III and VI of *Marlborough: His Life and Times,* pages 315, 648; Volumes I and V of *The World Crisis,* pages 2, 3, 483 are reprinted with permission of Charles Scribner's Sons. Copyright 1932, Charles Scribner's Sons; renewal copyright © 1960 Winston S. Churchill. Copyright 1930 Charles Scribner's Sons; renewal copyright © 1958 Winston Churchill. Copyright 1934, 1935 Charles Scribner's Sons; renewal copyright © 1962, 1963 Winston S. Churchill. Copyright 1938 Charles Scribner's Sons. Copyright 1923 Charles Scribner's Sons; renewal copyright © 1951 Winston S. Churchill. Copyright 1929 Charles Scribner's Sons; renewal copyright © 1957 Winston S. Churchill.

Houghton Mifflin Company has permitted use of material from Churchill's *The Second World War: The Gathering Storm, Their Finest Hour, The Hinge of Fate,* and *Triumph and Tragedy.*

Harcourt, Brace & World, Inc., has permitted use of material from Churchill's *Frontiers and Wars.*

Selections from *Churchill by His Contemporaries,* edited by Charles Eade, are reprinted by permission of Simon and Schuster, Inc.

Library of Congress Catalogue Card Number: 65–18320